CW00926518

Simon Dolan is one of entrepreneurs. As CEO of SJD Group Ltd, a business he founded in 1992 and expanded across the UK, he turns over £70 million a year and is regularly featured on the *Sunday Times* Rich List.

Simon continues to work his Midas touch across a range of industries, and has expanded his empire to include profitable magazines and websites, an airline and a motor-racing team. As a keen motor-racing driver, he formed the companies Jota Sport and The Drivers Club to offer private, high-performance driver training and driving events. Jota Sport is a highly successful sports car-racing outfit for which Simon drives at all major events.

Simon is also a one-time champion kick-boxer and a self-styled 'business angel'. Having established a £5 million fund to invest in new businesses, Simon gained national media coverage in 2010 for becoming the world's first 'Twitter Dragon', inviting pitches from entrepreneurs via 140-character 'tweets'.

SJD Accountancy has won a raft of awards, including 'Extraordinary Three Star Status' in the *Sunday Times* Best Companies Accreditation since 2007, and '*Sunday Times* Best Small Companies to Work For' Award in 2009 and 2007.

HOW TO MAKE
MILLIONS WITHOUT
A DEGREE

SIMON DOLAN

Matador
5 Weir Road
Kibworth Beauchamp
Leicester LE8 0LQ, UK
Tel: 0116 279 2277
Email: books@troubador.co.uk
Web: www.troubador.co.uk/matador

ISBN 9781848765900

British Library Cataloguing in Publication Data.
A catalogue record for this book is available from the British Library.

Printed in the UK by TJ International Ltd, Padstow, Cornwall

Matador is an imprint of Troubador Publishing Ltd

For my beautiful wife Sabrina,
and my gorgeous boys Bowie and Enzo.
Nothing means anything without you all by my side xxx

CONTENTS

PART 3

INTRODUCTION

By my 23rd birthday I'd hit the buffers. I'd left school at 16, cruised through a diploma at a local college, had various sales jobs, including selling timeshares, and received a drink driving ban. Unemployed, on the dole, with few prospects and fewer ideas, I was pretty much washed up, no doubt a disappointment and worry for my honest, hard-working parents. Then, driven more by desperation than anything, I started a simple business doing accounts and tax returns for small, local firms. I was good at it. Also, my work experience before and after leaving school turned out to be very relevant. My business grew, and quickly. Now, 17 years later, I own a group of companies turning over £70 million.

The funny thing is, while I'm proud of the way things turned out, and while it is a business success tale by any measure, it's not a remarkable story. I didn't invent some amazing gadget, struggle heroically against the odds or devise some revolutionary set of new business principles. And I didn't train for years, taking qualification after qualification, A levels, degree, masters degree... I started an ordinary business, grew it along old-fashioned lines – if a bit erratically on occasion – made my share of the usual mistakes and generally put in the slog.

I'm now the owner of a group of companies turning over £70 million. I'm the only shareholder, so the profits are mine to do what I like with. It was actually very simple to get to this rather favourable position in life. Astonishingly simple. Much easier than going to lectures, studying for hours on end and taking exam after exam. I'm going to tell you how I did it, because maybe you'd like to do it too.

I decided to write this book to shed light on the great 'mystery' of starting a business and earning a lot of money. At first I wondered if maybe I should wrap my story in mystery, work up some tricky formula that, if you follow it, would guarantee your passage to successful entrepreneurship and fabulous wealth, and if you didn't get rich it was because you didn't follow my instructions *carefully enough*, because you *missed out* some small but essential bit, or because you *didn't fully understand* this part or that part. But if I did that I'd be a bit of a con artist, because it's not true. The fact is I just drifted into something I had an aptitude for, saw that nobody else was doing it the way I was, did it well, and, after a while, got organised. I also got a bit lucky at one point later on, but if I hadn't done all the bits before that, the stroke of luck wouldn't have meant a bean. 'Luck is preparation multiplied by opportunity.'

I decided to write this book, not to share some unbelievable success story, but to show you that success isn't all that difficult if you follow a few simple rules. I'd like to show you how easy it is to start a business and do well, with or without a degree. So I'm just going to tell you how I did it, and focus on the parts which I know for a fact you can transfer to any sort of business to make it successful.

We're bombarded with news about the gaping budget deficit in this country, but I believe there is a more serious sort of deficit looming, one that saps our independence and enjoyment of life and threatens our country's future. It's a deficit of entrepreneurship. A deficit of initiative.

For the last 30 years or so, young people have been aggressively pushed onto an academic path leading to a university degree and entrepreneurship has been ignored. In the 1960s, the percentage of young people going to university was five per cent. These were the people training to be doctors and lawyers and priests and engineers and poets and naval officers and whatever else you needed a degree to do. Today that figure is closer to 45 per cent, and rising fast. And the government's target had been for 50 per cent of school leavers to go to university.

Why do we think getting a degree is so great? Because we're told that people with degrees have far better prospects. They get better jobs, better husbands and wives, cultivate healthier habits and are generally more successful. Whereas people who don't get degrees are poorer and get stuck in crummy, dead-end jobs and are at higher risk of becoming total losers and dropping out and burdening the state. As a nation, we worship nervously at the altar of higher education because we think it will equip people to become effective system surfers.

It's time to explode this myth. Actually, it's already exploded. It's pretty much an open secret now that many degrees are useless when it comes to getting a good job, and graduates are the first to admit it. A growing number of them end up in crummy jobs anyway, as well as being £20,000 in debt and, more worryingly, three to five years behind where they might have been in picking up solid skills and experience in the world of work.

I'm not going to overload you with statistics, but I couldn't resist this one: small and medium-size businesses account for 99 per cent of all companies in the UK and for three-fifths of private sector employment. This is where the jobs are. In a survey by the Centre for Enterprise conducted in 2010, most of them said they hired according to skill and experience, not academic qualifications, and 39 per cent said they *didn't need* graduate level skills in their business *at all*. Yet wave after wave of ambitious people still head off to university, like kamikaze pilots, with a sort of helpless shrug. But what else are they to do? What sane person would buck the trend and decide not to go to university, given the widespread acceptance that higher education offers everyone a better future?

I believe we're long overdue a good, alternative vision for education. Learning doesn't just take place in the classroom or lecture theatre. Why do people who show ability immediately get marked out for academia? And on the flip side, why are millions of people made to feel thick because they don't respond well to classroom learning and don't see the point of it? The tragedy is that many people will never come close to reaching their potential because they think they're stupid. It's such a waste.

What Happened to Good, Old-Fashioned Enterprise?

I wanted to write this book because if my story shows anything it's that anybody can become an entrepreneur – with or without a degree. It's time to 'big-up' entrepreneurship. We've lost the sense of it. Our default setting is: 'Got to get a job.' Hence the lemming-like rush to university. We nervously watch for government cuts and look at big corporations as the only wealth creators out there, when actually each one of us is a wealth creator. We're just collectively hobbled by a mindset of dependency.

What's more, entrepreneurship is something we either demonise or idealise. We demonise it because we've got a dysfunctional attitude to money. I call it dysfunctional because, while everyone craves money and the security and fun it brings, we don't trust or admire anyone who makes a point of actually getting a lot of it. We think the bald pursuit of wealth is an inferior goal, morally and intellectually (though we keep buying lottery tickets). People who set out to get rich are seen as shallow and grasping. Nobody wants to be thought of as *money-grabbing*, do they?

On the other hand, successful entrepreneurs are idealised, made into monumentally driven or gifted visionaries – freaks of nature, in other words. There are whole studies devoted to the psychological make-up of entrepreneurs. One even claimed to prove the entrepreneurial drive is *genetic*. And TV shows like *Dragon's Den* just stoke this totally false sense of hype and glory.

So if there is a 'big mysterious secret' in this book, it's this: You can start your own business and get rich – without going to university. Whatever you're doing now, whether you're a call-centre operative, house husband, lollipop person, waitress, company director, burger flipper or school-dropout, you can do it. Being an entrepreneur is not about entering some hellish gulag of slog, panic and financial ruin. Yes, plenty of start-ups fail, but you're less likely to if you read this book. Also, never forget that failure is good. Failure is as close as you're going to get to an iron-clad guarantee of success – next time. But there's good failure and bad failure, and I'll tell you everything I know about both.

I believe that everybody can become a successful entrepreneur. However, I am realistic and know that most people won't – not because they lack the resources, but some people simply prefer the security of employment, some feel that starting a business and getting rich is beneath them and sadly some people are just plain lazy.

But there's a whole other chunk of the population out there, mouldering away at work, frequently uttering to themselves those three, devastating little words: *Is this it?* And to them I say three little words back: *No it isn't.*

Maybe your job right now is exciting or commands respect. You may be a lawyer working 70-hour weeks for £80k a year. Or a director in a successful company. Or a social worker or nurse with dark rings under your eyes from bureaucracy and overwork, or a teacher struggling daily to impart some scraps of knowledge to a roomful of yobs. Or you may be a shopkeeper watching customers decamp one by one to the Tesco out by the roundabout.

Whatever your job right now, I bet from time to time you ask: Is this it? Why am I *doing* this? Who am I doing it *for*? You sense that the real action has somehow moved on to someplace else. What's the 'real action'? The 'real action' is the feeling you used to have when the sense of your own potential matched up favourably with the developing reality around you. The freshly-articled lawyer with six big firms fawning over you. The director with your own new division to grow. The teacher on the first day of school, and the social worker who just helped their first neglected kid.

Remember that feeling?

There is a great word in Buddhism: *Dukkha*. It means a

whole load of stuff, too much to go into here, but it includes that pervasive sense of dissatisfaction and restlessness we feel for no good reason. *Dukkha*. Disquietude. When the joy of the good times starts evaporating before they're even over. When you've got everything you need and you can supply everything your children need but it's still, somehow, *not enough*. Tell me you've never felt it. *Dukkha*.

Buddhists prescribe for this a lifelong journey of meditation, a search for enlightenment that has no practical end point.

If that's what spins your wheels, go for it. If not, I have another suggestion. Forget about getting a degree, if you don't already have one. If you do have one, stop telling yourself it can do things for you. Get back to where the real action is. Get back to having a good time. Get back to where your potential matches up to the developing reality. Get back to where you once belonged and **start running a business**.

Maybe you've already started down the entrepreneurial road. Maybe the business is up and running, but the lustre's gone. Maybe you think you've pushed it as far as it can go, or you're saddled with a deadbeat partner, or the market you're in has gone sour and the road ahead looks dreary. Maybe you're thinking you'd rather just go get some job because you could do without all the hassle. Danger! Don't! You can get it back. This book is for you, too. This book is for you, especially.

Do you want to regain that feeling of intense engagement? Of passionate drive? Where your senses are sharp, your mind is alert and your imagination is running wild? Where you're learning masses week in, week out? Or maybe you've never felt that and you want to start. The best way I know of doing that – legally and long-term – is by starting a business. And getting rich.

If you're under pressure to go to university, or perhaps are already working and feel like a failure because you don't already have a degree, I want to encourage you to starting doubting the sanctity of higher education. Is three years at university really necessary for you to lead a fulfilling, productive, independent life?

Er, no.

I believe that the university treadmill can actually be harmful. I think it deadens some people, robs them of confidence and fosters the mindset of job dependency.

I left school at 16. Or rather, I was asked to leave. That's because I was just messing around, and I was just messing around because I thought school was stupid.

And it was. For me, and for a lot of people, school is stupid so stretching it out for another two years at college, and three years at university, is even more stupid.

Even though I didn't go to university, I'm fairly wealthy, have a great life and create lots of jobs for other people. I also do civilised things like play Beethoven on the piano, strum my guitar from time to time and speak other languages (all of which I learned AFTER I left school by the way). I read lots of books and race some of the fastest cars on earth. Many of the most successful people in Britain don't have *any* academic qualifications, let alone a degree – you can read about them in part two of this book. For some people, *not* going to university can be the best career choice. It certainly was my best career choice.

I'm not suggesting that all education is pointless. Certainly basic schooling is really important, but for some people only up to a point. But if you're skilled at reading, reasonably numerate and have a handle on your basic weights and measures, you should start exploring the vast array of productive, non-educational activities (sometimes referred to as 'jobs') through which you can begin getting a life. Then, because you don't want to be mouldering away in some soul destroying job forever, start exploring the ideas in this book in case you too are entrepreneurial material – which I believe you are.

I hope you have as much fun reading this book as I did writing it. For me it's not just about getting rich without a degree, but living life with a sense of passion and engagement, where your senses are sharp, your mind is alert and your imagination is running wild. The best way I know of doing that – legally and long-term – is by starting a business.

PART 1

How I Dropped Out and Still Made It

CHAPTER ONE

My Days in the Classroom

My dislike of classroom learning took root long before Mr. Palmly's forehand smash to the head sent me flying backwards over my desk. Long before. I hated secondary school from the first day. King Edward VI Grammar in Chelmsford.

At primary school, I'd been OK with classroom learning. I'd been top of the class in good old readin', writin' and 'rithmetic. In fact I was the only one in my year to pass the eleven plus, which was why I'd got into King Edward VI (let's call it KEGS) in the first place. But in secondary school I couldn't work out why I had to learn what I had to learn. Chemistry, Physics, Biology, Geography, French, English Literature, History, Music, Religion, Latin... *Latin*? I just couldn't see the point.

But like I said, for me it soured on the first day. I'd never seen a grown man scream before. I'd seen ladies scream on television, like Faye Ray in the hairy fist of King Kong, but not a large, live man in the same room as me, screaming. In fury. At us. At me. I was addled with terror. Have you ever been addled with terror? It's when for a couple of seconds your brain can't actually process the incoming data. There is a sensation of cerebral vibration. Your eyes are wide open but your vision is strangely dim. Adrenalin floods your heart and you're a hair-trigger away from fight or flight. Isn't that a nice way to start your first day in big school?

Within those few seconds some of my quicker-thinking classmates had figured out what the trouble was and were standing by their desks. This caught on and we learned our first lesson: stand up when a Master enters the room.

That particular Master didn't actually hit us. His preferred method of intimidation was to stand very close to you, as in 'can't actually get any closer without the police being involved', bend his head down at right angles to his spine and bellow down into your upturned face.

Enough! Anybody over 30 has stories about teachers who these days would be arrested – or sectioned – well before the autumn half-term.

But no, wait. Here's one more. I didn't like music class. Later I would go on and teach myself guitar and piano, but back then I had no interest. So one day I was goofing around at the back of the music room with Howard, my mate, when the music teacher, whose name escapes me just now, picked up a cymbal and threw it at us. Like a Frisbee. That really stuck in my head. Not the cymbal, thankfully, but the fact that he threw it. Fortunately he missed, and nine pounds of razor-edged, Zildjian bronze zinged past us and crashed resoundingly against the wall. And then resoundingly onto the floor.

Like I said at the start though, the reason I hated secondary school was not because of all this casual brutality and general nuttiness – it was because I couldn't see the point of all the subjects we had to learn. No one explained it to me. Why was I learning Latin?

Latin!

Why?

The question started bugging me right away, and nobody would tell me the answer. The real one, anyway. I know the answer now. The answer is this: 'These are the hoops you must jump through for the next seven years and for at least another three after that if you prove yourself worthy of university. And you must jump through these hoops, Grasshopper, because otherwise you will be reviled by society, you will live with your parents well into middle age, and you will end your days a vomit-encrusted, purse-snatching crack-head. Or worse, you will work in the civil service.'

That's the real answer. That's the great, dark bogeyman of

our time. I wish somebody had told me. I could maybe have understood *that*. It's completely wrong, but at least it's honest and, who knows, I might even have gone along with it. Which would have been a tragedy.

As it happens I did not go along with it. I wish I could say I went out in a blaze of glory, but it was actually just a damp fizzle after five years of sniggering, teenage neglect. At KEGS we had to do O levels (that's what they called GCSEs in the olden days) one year earlier than other schools. As well as the compulsory ones like Maths, English, RE, Latin, German, etc., we could choose two others. I chose Art, which I reckoned would be a doddle, and Ancient Greek, because nobody had ever failed the Ancient Greek O level at KEGS. The reason for this was that only six people had ever taken it. With class sizes maxing out at one, the Greek Master was pretty much honour-bound to accept a pass-rate of nothing less than 100 per cent. In that first tranche of ten or twelve O levels I passed four, including Ancient Greek. I find I can still conjugate 'the' in that fine, dead language. The others were English Language, English Literature and Maths. I failed Art.

The next year we were expected to spend mopping up yet more O levels before starting A levels. There were guys getting 16 or 17 O levels at KEGS, and this was when O levels meant something. I took six more, sticking to the 'lighter' subjects, Environmental Studies, Economics, that sort of thing. Other people may have found their abysmal performance in the first lot somehow sobering. You'd have thought certain lessons might have been learned. They weren't. I just couldn't be bothered. I failed them all.

I have what has been termed a 'constructive' personality. Basically it means I can't be bothered to do anything if I don't see the point of it. It's an aspect of my character I've learned to temper because, taken to its extreme, it can render all sorts of things 'pointless': basic politeness, communication with other human beings, washing, even getting out of bed. Throughout those years, for instance, I was great at rugby and football, which was probably why I wasn't kicked out. The point of sport was obvious to me: it was really fun.

So after my results were in, just before my 16th birthday, the deputy head at KEGS called me in for a little chat. Not unkindly, he asked me if I'd given any thought as to what I'd be doing next term. I hadn't given it any thought whatsoever, but said I was thinking about doing some A levels. English and, uh… stuff.

'How interesting,' he said. 'And where are you thinking of doing those?'

I didn't understand the question. 'Here,' I said.

He chuckled at this. Quite a bit. He found it really amusing.

'Oh no, my dear boy. Ho ho ho. I'm afraid you won't be coming back here.'

I was being asked to leave.

CHAPTER TWO

The School of Cheese and Eggs: My Real Education

Was I upset? No. Were my parents? I can't remember. We had plenty of rows, but they were more about me being a teenager than about school, specifically. I can remember one in particular after I dyed my hair blond. I did that, copying my all-time hero, David Bowie, to demonstrate my uncompromising non-conformism, along with millions of other non-conformist teenagers.

No I wasn't really upset, partly because I had plenty of other things to do. For instance, I happened to be coining it in, thanks to my mum. Once my sister and I were off at school, my mother started going out to work, first at the local hospital and later qualifying as an occupational therapist. Ever attuned to the therapeutic benefits of keeping occupied, she was always getting me jobs.

'Simon, I found a job for you', was a current refrain.

The first of these was delivering newspapers to people in the hospital. I didn't like that job. Taking money from the limp or shaking hands of sick people was horrible. Then she got me a job at a local garage tidying up after the mechanic. I got three quid if I worked a half day and five quid for a whole day. This was pretty big money for a 12-year-old. Plus I got a lift home on the back of the mechanic's motorcycle. My career as an oily rag would never quite achieve lift-off, however. The guy was a bit sporadic in showing up for work on Saturdays, and not long after my mum came home with an even better job: working at an eggs and cheese stall at Chelmsford Market.

You wouldn't think it, but there's a lot of money in cheese and eggs. My employer was a guy called Mark, who'd learned the dark art of the cheese and eggs business while working as a buyer for the big food wholesaler, Danish Bacon. Once he saw how it all worked, he struck out on his own. He put in long hours. His day would start with pick-ups from suppliers, or from a big refrigerated lock-up he kept out of town, and he'd be on site by five-thirty to set up. That's when I'd have to be there too, putting the tables together and laying out the plastic green grass. It was a long day but I got twenty pounds for it. These days you wouldn't be allowed to wear out poor little boys like that. I worked Saturdays and, during school holidays, Tuesdays and Fridays as well. Sixty pounds a week! That's quite a disposable income for a 14-year-old, even by today's standards. Mark could afford to pay me that though, because he was taking home a thousand a week at least.

I learned a lot over four years working alongside Mark and watching him closely. He was a nice guy, not that much older than me. In his early twenties, I guess, energetic, fun and successful with the ladies. And he trusted me. I'd like to do a fancy PowerPoint presentation to demonstrate the value of life experience over lessons in the classroom, but I can't – so I'll settle for a good, old-fashioned list.

1. Amazing mental arithmetic: Mark didn't use a till. This was no problem with the eggs – you just added up the price per dozen. But cheese is a different story. Cheese is a whole different kettle of fish. Say Mrs Smith was having a party and wanted to offer her guests a cheese board. She needs eight different cheeses, in different quantities, all with a different price per pound. There is no calculator and a queue is building up. I got quite good at that.

2. Charm: As a boy I was a shy, introverted person. But by watching Mark, I was initiated into the mysteries of customer rapport. At a time when most teenagers'

vocabularies do not extend much beyond 'Wha'?', 'Yuh', and 'Nice one', I was reeling off the patter like a goodun'. 'Hello Mrs Smith! You're looking marvellous today Mrs Smith! Is that a new outfit, Mrs Smith?' They love it, customers: friendliness. And it did wonders for my technique with girls, in which I was starting to take a keen interest. On Saturdays there was usually a clutch of them hanging around the stall, though whether it was me or the manly Mark that drew them I can't quite remember. Anyway, I found I could adopt this whole new persona. After a day of sizzling banter I'd be riding my bike home feeling large and buzzing practically the whole journey.

3. Responsibility: This is probably the biggest thing we want teenagers to learn, isn't it? That the things they do have consequences, and to begin to predict, and then manage, those consequences. There was one girl who lived near me that I took a particular interest in, and I started 'accidentally' missing my bus so I could take the later one she was on. After being late just once Mark pulled me aside and said, simply: 'Simon, you're no use to me if you're not going to show up on time.' Ow! That got my attention. There would be no exam retakes or cosy 'pull your socks up' chats. This was the real world. I'd lose this excellent job. I was never late again.

CHAPTER THREE

David Bowie and the Art of Getting On With It

It was around the time when I was apprenticing as a cheese and eggs guy that I discovered my first true master. I found a blank cassette lying around, reeled halfway through. Suspecting it was some cast-off wizardry from my older sister, I popped it in my 'boom box' and pressed play just in time to get a tuba blast, followed by this finicky, grating, androgynous voice singing about Major Tom in a spaceship. I finished listening, and then rewound to the beginning. I did that again and again. I could hardly believe what I was hearing.

Cast your mind back, if you can, to the ambient sound of late '82, early '83. KC and the Sunshine Band, Wham!, Lionel Richie (Hello), Frankie Goes to Hollywood (Relax), Billy Joel (Uptown Girl), Duran Duran, Culture Club (Do You Really Want to Hurt Me?)... *yes, very much*. It was a musical era dominated by schmaltz. Saccharine, derivative schmaltz. But this! It felt like a strange new element for the periodic table of music. I had no idea what this guy was doing, but he sure seemed to.

It was, of course, 'Space Oddity'. I'd discovered David Bowie – 14 years after the fact. I had some catching up to do. I had 16 albums plus at least three greatest hits compilations to locate, purchase and devour. There were also 11 biographies by that point, each of which needed finding, buying and reading. There were the illustrated discographies, unofficial tour chronicles, the videos, the bootleg recordings, three feature films and the dozen or so songbooks published by then. And, of course, my first guitar (You can see where all the eggs and cheese money went).

Why did I like Bowie so much? If you know a Bowie song or two and like them, there is no need to explain. If you don't know Bowie or don't like him, I'll try – briefly. To my mind, he is everything that a full-blown stadium rock act does, everything that a dulcet-toned, guitar-thrumming maiden does, everything that an edgy, weird comedian does in a smoke-filled club in New York, everything… etc. Anyway, it's all there, whizzed up in a blender and painted by a mad scientist on twelve inches of vinyl. There's no formula. It's never the same. And yet it's always Bowie.

But it wasn't just the music I loved. The Bowie story is amazing. His drive to become Earth's most enduringly successful pop star taught me a lesson that's with me today, a lesson that I will encapsulate with a nifty acronym: GOWI. Get On With It. The stuff you want to do, get on with it! And nobody did GOWI like Bowie.

Bowie and GOWI

Born little Davie Jones in 1947, Bowie had no leg-up whatsoever in the world of pop. His parents were nobodies. The family moved to a cramped terraced house in Bromley, a crashingly dull suburb close neither to London nor to proper countryside, full of your usual commuting, nine-to-five types of people.

But this cat wanted to be a pop star.

It was Little Richard what did it for him. 1955. Up to then it had all been his mum warbling along to the BBC Light Programme on the wireless, but in '55 he turned the dial and… *A-wop-bop-a-loo-bop, A-lop-bam-boom!* He was eight, and his destiny was sealed. He goofed around in school – *just like me.* Except he did it better. He *failed* his eleven plus and got sent to the local slave hatchery, Bromley Technical High School. In those days, if you failed your eleven plus it was highly unlikely you'd go on to study a degree. He got a job as a delivery boy for a local butcher (echoes of eggs and cheese there?) and with his earnings bought a white, plastic saxophone, which he proceeded to become not very good at. (Later he proceeded also to become not very good at guitar and piano.) He got his first band together in 1962, when he was 15. They were called The Konrads and their first gig was at the Bromley Tech school fete, playing a few Shadows covers. In 1963 he left Bromley Tech with one O level, in Art.

Thus, staunchly girded with qualifications, he got on with his destiny (Oh, and he took one more thing from Bromley Tech that would prove invaluable to his otherworldly image later – one permanently dilated pupil, an injury resulting from a schoolyard fight over a girl). He didn't hang around in the education system, trying desperately to get enough grades together to go to university.

He got a job, an office drone job, and every spare moment he and The Konrads rehearsed and played gigs at church halls and youth clubs around Bromley. They even marched up to Decca Studios in London to record their first song, which was never released. Bowie left The Konrads in 1964 because he wanted to play edgier R&B material, and formed Davie Jones and the King Bees, him on sax and vocals. He was impatient for stardom. After all, at 17 he was getting on a bit.

But fame was taking its cruel time. In 1964, Bowie left the Bees and formed The Mannish Boys, with him again on sax and vocals, playing high-energy, electric, bluesy, utterly formulaic rock. In their early recordings it doesn't even sound like Bowie. By the end of the year, The Mannish Boys were working hard, gigging two or three nights a week and venturing beyond Bromley to the Medway towns –and even to bars and clubs in London and Essex. They were also auditioning regularly for spots on television. At this stage, Bowie quit the one real job he would ever have. He was also still living in his Bromley bedroom.

This period might sound kind of glamorous but anybody who has ever played in a band will know the truth: that for every knicker-flinging mosh-fest of glory there are umpteen dud gigs.

Dud gigs are the bread-and-butter tedium of starting out. You load all the gear: drums, amps, speakers, cables, etc., drive an hour and a half in a clapped out van with a bunch of people you're probably sick of by now, find the grotty little pub, unload everything, set up, tune, sound check, get abused by the alcoholic landlady, play two sets of songs you're bored of to a gaggle of sullen yobs, tear everything down, argue with the landlady over getting paid, load up the van again and sit in it, squabbling, for the hour-and-a-half back home.

But for Davie Jones it didn't matter. He was Getting On With It! He had no choice.

In December the Mannish Boys hit the big time, winning a supporting spot for a six-date tour with Gerry and the Pacemakers as the headline act. Sharing the bill were Gene Pitney, Marianne Faithful, Bobby Shafto with The Roofraisers (whoever they were) and The Kinks, who, after their first two singles bombed, were flush with the success of 'You Really Got Me'.

Imagine how it would have been for those guys. Up to then, Margate would have been an exotic road trip for The Mannish Boys. Now they were playing Wigan, Hull, Edinburgh, Stockton-on-Tees, Newcastle and Scarborough alongside established names, both on the performing and producing side. I've played in a band. If there existed something equivalent to a doctorate in pop performance those six days would be it.

And Davie Jones hadn't even hit 18 yet.

CHAPTER FOUR

Messing Around, Jail and the Big Idea

My Messing Around Phase

An important part of Getting On With It is the preliminary self-directed Messing Around phase. This is perhaps what university robs people of – a good few years right at the bottom of the ladder, learning how the real world works.

Bowie's Messing Around phase was quite short. He had an uncommon degree of focus. I would like to say that there are strong parallels between this period in Bowie's life and mine, but that would be a gross misrepresentation of the facts. I did play in a band. We called ourselves, with more prophetic accuracy than irony, The Unknown. We played six gigs. What artistic tension there was in the band came mostly from a divergence of opinion as to how many Bowie songs we should cover. I was way out on one end of that spectrum of opinion, and everybody else was way out on the other. It was a lot of fun, but as a band, as I said, our destiny was pretty much summed up in our name.

Eggs and cheese, meanwhile, were doing fine but… well… you know – eggs and cheese? What I'm trying to say is that, for whatever reason, the whole eggs-n-cheese-n-rock-n-roll nexus was beginning to lose some of the power it had in the weeks after I got kicked out of KEGS. Or maybe it was just that I wasn't quite ready. Or maybe I didn't know how to start. Anyway, it was my mum, I think, who suggested the local college in Chelmsford – Dovedales. She pointed out that they offered a diploma in

Business and Finance. Business and Finance… hmmm. I didn't know why, but there was something about that I liked the sound of.

So that's where I went.

Here was an altogether different experience of education. After the general lunacy of KEGS, college felt all rather grown up and easy going. It wasn't stuffy in the least. And it wasn't pointless. People were nice. You didn't have to call lecturers Master. The subjects were reasonably interesting and designed to be applicable: computing, accounts, general running-a-company stuff. How to make money. I liked it. And there were girls. So those were good years, from the ages of 16 to 18. In my spare time I fooled around with The Unknown and slung cheese and eggs. I got a BTech qualification and notched up a few formative experiences, mostly with girls.

Then my dad got a job in Manchester, which meant he and Mum were moving. I was at a loose end. Actually, a girl I was involved with at the time, who was very academically inclined, had been accepted to study Chemistry at Imperial College, London. The inevitable happened. She dumped me. So I went with them. It was sad to leave the profitable world of eggs and cheese behind, but I'd learned plenty from Mark and at that stage I was mostly interested in music anyway. I did briefly research the idea of running my own cheese and egg stall in Manchester with the help of Mark. It all seemed like a great idea until I started talking to some of the stall holders in less than salubrious Manchester markets – apparently market pitches would generally change hands due to the threat of violence more than your more traditional waiting list, and at that point in my life kickboxing wasn't even on the agenda. So, cheese and eggs were sadly no more.

I needed to find a job in Manchester, so, given my interest in music, I decided to write letters to all the recording studios in the Manchester area. I thought maybe I could be like Tony Visconti, the genius American who produced for T. Rex, Thin Lizzy, Adam Ant, The Stranglers and, of course, Bowie. I got, to quote somebody Visconti didn't produce, no reply at all. That's when Dad, ever on hand with the squarest advice possible, suggested that with my BTech in Business and Finance, I might as well check out a few accounting firms. That's right: accounting firms. I stared at my National Diploma and the horrible suspicion dawned that I had fallen into an evil trap designed to turn me into my father. A bit like Frank Sinatra in *The Manchurian Candidate*, where this all-American army officer has been secretly hypnotised by the evil Communists and programmed to be an assassin. Could even the girls of Dovedales College have been party to it?

I decided to try one accounting firm. One. I saw an ad in the paper, a post advertised by the accountancy firm, Uppal and Warr. I didn't actually use my left hand, but it was the briefest, hastiest, scrawling letter I'd ever written. Yet the next day they were on the phone inviting me in for an interview.

Cursing, I went and fairly briskly brought the conversation round to the salary they were offering. It was £50 a week. Of the two of us in that quiet room only I found this hilarious. I was making £60 for a three-day week when I was 14! Despite my sense of humour I was offered the job then and there. I went home fuming. It was so unfair! Mum and Dad urged me to look into their eyes, suggested I was getting sleepy, and pointed out that, with my room and board covered, it was as good a job as any other.

So began my Messing Around phase proper. This is a key phase in the entrepreneur's life. It's when you're not in full-time education anymore, but nor are you in full-blown GOWI mode, because you haven't yet found the 'It' you're supposed to be getting on with. The classic Messing Around phase can last anywhere from a few months to several years. Some people never get out of the Messing Around phase. Generally it's typified by seemingly dead-end jobs or hair-brained, non-profit adventures. The 'fun-but-ultimately-meaningless' quotient is usually quite high. Occasionally the Messing Around phase might include the 'yet-another-degree' ploy, but not often. Unlike 'yet-another-degree', the Messing Around phase is only superficially a waste of time. That's because most of the experience gathered while messing around is ultimately useful. You might say my two years at Dovedales could be classed as part of the phase, but I don't think so. Anyway, I'll leave that to the Messing Around theorists.

So, I began working at Uppal and Warr. And there is no easy way of saying this, but… it was fine. It all just clicked. Some people find numbers scary, but for me accounts and tax returns were a kind of comfort zone. It was simple, useful work and I was pretty good at it. And before too long I was making better money. During busy periods Tim, the guy who owned the company, would contract me to come in on weekends to get through the workload, and he'd pay me 20 per cent of his fees. After a year there I was bringing home £120 a week. I was 19.

Then my dad got a better job down south so my parents started preparing to move again. I was reluctant to go with them, not because I was dedicated to Uppal and Warr, but because I had a particularly cute and imaginative girlfriend at the time. It was pretty obvious that the time was ripe for striking out on my own. So I bought a house. I found this remarkably easy to do, especially since Tim helped me organise a 100 per cent, interest-only mortgage. It was a little two-bed terraced affair in Denton, an area of Manchester with which I failed to form any lasting bonds. Denton is notable for three things. One, Mick Hucknall, the Simply Red guy, was from there. Two, it was next to Hyde, where Dr. Harold Shipman had his surgery. Three, it was also next to Hattersley, where Ian Brady and Myra Hindley lived.

Anyway, it was a house, and I was the man of it. How cool was that?

Learning the Hard Way – but Learning!

A key characteristic of the entrepreneur's Messing Around phase is *Situational Multiplicity*. That's the technical term for doing a bunch of stuff. You can't just sit around for years in one job. There needs to be a pattern of grip and release or you don't cram in enough experience and general pointlessness, which is essential for building the necessary head of motivational steam. So a correct instinct in me stirred one day and I walked into Tim's office and gave him the pay-me-more-or-I-walk speech. After several months of hard slog, I felt I deserved more money. I genuinely thought Tim would agree. After all, I wasn't asking for a *lot* more money, just a raise in line with the money I believed I was earning the company.

It was a shock when Tim, ever the astute businessman, pointed out where the door was.

I walked.

I don't want to sound too brave about this, as really I didn't have a lot of choice. I'd fully expected Tim to boost my salary rather than boot me out, so it was a nasty surprise to find myself out on the street. I began looking for another job.

What fun!

It was then I saw an astounding ad in the paper. It was for a sales job, and successful candidates stood to earn £50,000 a year if they hit their targets. My heart began to pound. 'Damn it!' I thought. 'The paper was already a day old! They'd be swamped with applications!' There wasn't a moment to lose.

It turned out to be remarkably easy to get an interview. They were held in the lobby of a swanky hotel. I was interviewed by a guy I'll call Terry. He was great. Energetic, funny, a bit mad. He seemed to be more interested in basic vital signs than anything else. He gave a spiel. The job was selling holiday timeshares. I'd never heard of it before, but it sounded like a great idea.

'How does that sound,' he asked.

'Like a great idea,' I said.

He beamed at me.

'You've got yourself a job, son.'

It wasn't a job, as such. I was to be self-employed, earning fabulous commissions. But first we had to be trained. For a couple of days Terry and some other high-flyers showed us the ropes. It was tremendously exciting. The company would buy databases (basically lists of names and addresses), and the people on these lists were sent letters telling them they'd won a prize, like a £200 holiday voucher – which would turn out to be valid only for such hotspots as Inuvik in the Spring, or Moldova – and all they had to do to claim their prize was come along to a 'brief presentation'. Our job, once we had a group of them sitting in a room, was to sell five or ten-year timeshare packages in Lanzarote.

Terry and the guys went through all the techniques and I lapped it up. I immersed myself in it. At the end of the first day Terry said he'd give £25 to whoever gave the best presentation in the morning. I practised late into the night, and in the morning everybody else was rubbish and I was brilliant. There was applause, and laughter.

'Good work,' said Terry.

'What about his 25 quid?' someone asked.

Terry looked uncomfortable and patted his pockets. I got a couple of grubby tenners, and he promised me the rest later. Something should have twigged then, but it didn't.

The work was a classic sales challenge. Short of blackmail and locking the doors you could do just about anything. I took to it like a duck to water. The trick, first off, was to get them to like you. That was key. We were taught cunning techniques. For instance, ask the potential customer (the 'UP' for 'Unqualified Prospect'), what they do for a living. People love talking about themselves, and they'll love you for asking. Even if they know deep down it's just a ploy, they'll still love you for asking.

'What do you do for a living, sir?'

It allows you to say, 'Is that right? You know I've always wanted to do that!' It makes them feel great and you all get along like a house on fire.

On one of my early tours I had this family: mum, dad, hulking grown son. Now, the people who actually showed up to the presentations were not generally the most twinkling stars in the firmament, but this family seemed to take dullness to uncharted levels.

'Before we go on, why don't you tell me a little about yourselves?' I said gamely. 'What do you do, sir?'

'O ahh beh-yek biskits [he baked biscuits, in the McVities plant].'

Finding myself with absolutely nothing to say to this, I just smiled and blinked a bit, my mouth opening and closing like a fish. So I turned to the son.

'And how about you? What do you do, sir.'

'O ahh beh-yek biskitsuzwell.'

What a grounding in sales!

I was ruthless and worked like a dog. We had Mondays off. On the other six days our first tour would be at 11 am, and the last of the day was at seven in the evening. You were encouraged to keep your group captive for as long as it took, grinding them down with sweet-talk, hysterical enthusiasm and aggressively narrowed logic. My last tour of the day often went on until 11 at night.

There is a great film called *Glengarry Glen Ross* about property salesmen in America. It shows how the human soul can be warped in an aggressive sales environment, and it is entirely accurate. One of the lines in that film is delivered by a mean bastard played by Alec Baldwin who is brought in to shake up an underperforming sales team. His message to them is 'ABC': Always Be Closing. All their skill, all their experience, their very humanity, is worth nothing unless they get the prospect to 'sign on the line that is dotted'. That's pretty much what it was like with the timeshares. Once we got into a conversation with some UPs, we had to introduce them right away to one of the senior guys, who would have a quick and friendly chat, and then we would melt away. This was called the 'tipover'. We did this because when it came down to the nitty gritty, the signing on the line that is dotted, the senior guy would parachute in with his superior closing skills.

I would say: 'Excellent Mr and Mrs Macguilly, now how would you prefer to pay the deposit on the £14,000? Cash or cheque is fine. Right now would be splendid.'

And they would say: '£14,000? You must be bloody joking!'

And I would say: 'Ah. I thought we'd agreed that was the

package that suited you best. You do have a chequebook with you?'

And they would say: 'Come on mother, get your coat.'

And I would say: 'Hmmm. If you'll just wait a second, I think there may be one very extra special package remaining for one very extra special couple. I'll just get my colleague Terry, whom you met earlier.'

And Terry would breeze over, all smiles, and start negotiating at £12k, then £10k, then £8k, and so on, until the Macguillys had been reeled in.

But it wasn't over then. Oh no. The Macguillys could not be allowed to leave without paying a deposit. This deposit could be anything, cheque, cash, an earring, anything. Without that there was no deal. Without that they would almost certainly back out once the fresh air of the outside hit their faces. We had an expression for people like these – they were punters coming on the 'be back' bus. It never arrived.

One evening I actually reached an agreement with a dazed couple myself. Jackpot! I couldn't believe it. *They* couldn't believe it. I struggled to remain calm. *ABC!* I had to close! I brought up the small matter of the deposit.

They shook their heads. 'We don't have any money on us.'

'That's no problem,' I said. 'A cheque will be fine.'

'We left our chequebook at home.'

'Not a problem. I'll come with you to your house and you can write a cheque and then we're all sorted!'

'We live in Liverpool.'

We were in Manchester. I thought quickly.

'Not a problem! I'll come with you to Liverpool, right now, and you can write a cheque and then we're all sorted!'

It was about 11 o'clock at night. This poor couple had nowhere to turn. We drove all the way from Manchester to Liverpool with me in the back, yammering away like an idiot. They wrote me a cheque and I got a cab back to Manchester. I had no money either so I wrote the cabbie a cheque.

The couple's cheque, of course, bounced, as did my cheque

to the cabbie. But it didn't matter, and nor did my lack of commission, because I had closed a deal!

After the 'tours' we salespeople would hit the bars until late, laughing about the amusing UPs, trading stories about the legendary wealth of the guys running the company, and speculating dreamily over when we might actually get paid. We didn't mind waiting. We were on the yellow brick road. *On target £50k!* We understood that you had to do 20 tours before you could even hope to get a sale. We understood that even after a deal was closed, it took time for the UP to get financing and for our commission to work its way down the pipeline to us. We ignored rumours that the higher-ups distorted final figures and creamed off the top. We got flung the odd bit of cash here and there to keep body and soul together, and we had credit cards.

We were living the dream!

It was exactly like a cult.

I slung those timeshares for six months solid, living on credit cards, credit cards and more credit cards. In essence, I borrowed every bit of cash I could to fund myself during this period. At the time I thought the investment was worth it – after all, those timeshares were going to make me unbelievably rich!

Then the inevitable happened. I woke up one morning to a shaft of revelatory light. This was a scam. I would never be paid. Fortunately my soul had not been permanently warped, so I simply stopped showing up. I just disappeared.

Whether the timeshare product was in any way valid or not I never did find out. I do know that various groups of miffed timeshare holders have sprung up, like the Lanzarote Beach Club Members' Association.

Jail Break

Onward. There was more messing around to be done. I went for a job selling photocopiers and fax machines. Throughout the interview I just sat there laughing and joking. Why, I'm not sure.

At the end the guy whose company it was, John Gibbon, sat back and said: 'I don't know whether to give you the job or not.'

'Why?' I asked.

'Because you're just sitting there grinning.'

'Well, what? Do you want me to be miserable?'

He gave me the job. It came with a car!

More classic sales stuff (an essential skill, by the way, and anybody who acquires it will not be out of a job for long. It will be essential for your business, too. They do not teach it in school). Every morning we were given a patch to cover and we'd go round to all the businesses in that patch asking if they wanted to buy a photocopier or a fax machine. Then we went back to the office and called them up. I did fairly well at this, and I was getting paid for it.

Every week there would be a sales meeting at which the poorest performer would be subjected to sustained ridicule and abuse, and then John would take us out to the pub. Then we'd go on to a nightclub, Mr. Smith's in Warrington, where we would subject our livers to sustained ridicule and abuse until three in the morning, and then we would dutifully drive home.

It was bound to happen, and it happened to me. I got done. I don't remember all that much about getting stopped and taken to the police station, but I remember sitting on a bed in a cell in my rumpled suit, feeling very distinctly that I did not like being there. Not one little bit. If I was going to be in a cubby hole, it would be because I wanted to be in said cubby hole. I felt that quite distinctly. I was quite pissed. Certain scenes kept playing through my mind. Well, one scene, actually. Very powerfully. It was the jail break scene in *First Blood*, where Rambo is arrested in some Hicksville town for vagrancy and gets taken down to the cells, where the cops go a little overboard in processing him. Tortured in 'Nam, Rambo goes berserk, overpowers 15 of them, breaks out of the building, hooks a guy off a motorcycle and roars off into the woods.

I stood up. The moment was now. I went to the door of the cell and pushed. To my amazement, it swung open. The dozy cops forgot to lock it! I had to move fast. Shuffling and burping stealthily, I made my way down a corridor, turned a corner, pushed through some double doors and found myself looking up and down a deserted street in the frosty Warrington night. Well, well. Stay calm, I told myself. In seconds there will be helicopters, searchlights, Warrington's finest in full body armour shouting 'ON THE FLOOR, MOTHERF@*&R!' I turned left and began to walk, gonging the odd signpost as I went. I needed a plan. My house was 40 miles away on the other side of Manchester. My car had been impounded. There were no motorcyclists to hook off. But I did have a mate, Ivor, who lived about two miles away. I'd go there and lie low.

It was exceedingly cold and it took a long time to cover those two miles. The feeling of exhilaration was giving way to a comprehensive headache. Eventually I got to Ivor's house and banged on the door. But he'd been with us at Mr. Smith's and was as pissed as me. I couldn't wake him up. I could wake up the people in the house on the left, and I could wake up the people in the house on the right, but I couldn't wake up Ivor. When the neighbours began talking about calling the police I decided to give up. I started walking again. It really was very cold. It had been quite a long day. What would Rambo have done? Rambo would have sniffed out the nearest park and fashioned a cloak out of the hides of 200 squirrels.

Unfortunately I had left my Bowie knife at home, and my toes were numb.

It took me a good hour to find the police station again. I went up to the cop behind a desk.

'Hi,' I said.

'Hi.'

'I was here earlier.'

'Yes. How can I help you?'

'I was in a cell.'

'Right.'

'But I left.'

'OK.'

'Can I go back in?'

But by then, they were full up. So I spent the rest of the night trying to sleep in a plastic chair in the waiting room, pestering them to breathalyse me every hour until I was fit to drive my sorry ass home.

Then, nothing happened. I knew it would take time for the letter to come with a court date, but a month went by. I kept selling fax machines and photocopiers. Then another month went by with me driving around with impunity. In the third month the fervent hope began to dawn that somehow my case had fallen through the cracks. By the end of that month I was giving the air discreet little punches. I bragged to a work-mate about it. He said that didn't sound right, which was not good at all because he had been to jail, properly, and knew the system. He had a friend who was a clerk in the Warrington Magistrates' Court and he gave her a call. That's when I learned about the warrant out for my arrest for failing to appear in court. I went and turned myself in to the police for the second time.

I was banned for 18 months.

Down with the Ship

John was really nice about it. Clearly I couldn't sell fax machines and photocopiers any more, but he did offer me a telesales job in Liverpool. This I declined. The situation just didn't feel that desperate. It never does when you're 21.

And so my Messing Around period entered the all-important chrysalis phase. I signed on. I mooched. I pottered. I learned how little effort it actually took to fill a day. By the time you've had breakfast, done some weight training, read *Weight Training Monthly*, had lunch, moseyed on down to the library for a nose about in the stacks, done some more weight training, had tea, etc., bam! The day is gone. If you wanted to fit in some television, snacking and a restorative nap, you actually had to be focused to a fairly high level.

Financially, my ship was taking its time going down. The orchestra kept playing. The shuffleboard pitch was busy. I was on the dole. I found a source of cheap fax machines, factory seconds, and made a bit of cash boxing them up and selling them as brand new in *Loot*. I had credit cards. The bank seemed pretty relaxed the first time I defaulted on the mortgage. Money-wise, my main concern at the time was scraping together enough to go down the pub on Friday nights.

It took a little over a year for the alarm bells in the engine room to finally reach me in my cosy wheelhouse. Eventually it sunk in once and for all that there was no room left on the credit cards and that the bank's next bit of correspondence would be chiefly about foreclosure. There was only one thing to do. Taking a strip out of a Captain Kneejerk comic, I went straight down to the newsagents and asked them to give me a job delivering papers. They laughed at me. Hmm, I thought. Maybe that wasn't the thing to do. I paused, and in that pause an idea came to me which, though I didn't know it at the time, would crack open the cocoon and let the Camberwell Beauty of Simon Dolan the entrepreneur emerge and take its first, tentative flaps.

I spent ten pounds on an ad in the paper saying I'd do end-of-year accounts for £99 and bookkeeping for ten pounds per month.

In interviews I have claimed that the ten pounds I paid for this ad was my last. While that sounds neat and dramatic it is not strictly true, because my last ten pounds, as in actual cash, had gone long before. I may have had a crack of leeway on one credit card or other, or I may have borrowed it, I can't quite remember. Anyway, the ad went in. And nothing happened. For three weeks I paced, watching the phone, checking the jack, picking up the receiver to see if there was a ring tone.

At the end of three weeks I got a call. It wasn't one of my mates goofing around. It wasn't the electricity company chasing the last two bills. It was a nervous-sounding woman who ran a flower shop. I didn't suppose I could do her accounts, did I? she concluded. I asked her to hold while I checked my diary. Slowly,

I turned a few pages of *Triceps* magazine. I made little noises of doubt and concern. Then I picked up the receiver and said that by a fantastic stroke of luck – a terrible bereavement for one of my regular clients – I just happened to be free *right now*.

That client meant I could put another ad in the paper, and not long after that I was away.

Of course, in GOWI terms I was way behind. At around about the same age – 22, say – David Bowie had already played upwards of a thousand gigs with at least five bands. He'd released several singles and two albums. He'd worked closely with four different managers, each of whom taught him masses about the pop business. He'd formed a mime and theatre troupe that flopped commercially but which developed his stage genius. And he'd established a tight network of friends, lovers and associates who were at the very centre of the hip London pop scene. In terms of Getting On With It, he'd wasted no time. Like I said, nobody did GOWI like Bowie.

However, after much messing around, I was at least finally GOWI in my own special way. And my Messing Around phrase had been very important. Vital, you could say. It had prepared the ground very well for my GOWI phase. I had a highly marketable skill. Tax returns evoke fear and loathing in many people, but I had somewhat of a natural ability for accounting and they came easily to me. A typical customer from this period would be a subcontractor, like a brickie or a spark (electrician). Doing their returns involved adding up all their tax receipts stuffed in one shopping bag and subtracting all their expenses stuffed in another shopping bag. I could do it in 20 minutes, and charge £99. When things got rolling I stood to make £297 an hour, and my overheads were nil. They were always due a refund of something like £1,500 or £2,000 so there was good feeling all round.

I was also, remember, a consummate salesman. That £99 figure for year-end accounts was actually the exception rather than the rule. For clients with more complex accounts, say a shop, I'd sit down with them and ask in a friendly sort of way if I could see their last year's tax return. They would go and get it. I would then go through the return looking for an important figure – what the accountant who filed this return had charged. It would be right there – £475, for instance – in bold. Now please don't think I was being dishonest by subtlety obtaining this figure. As a good salesperson, I simply wanted to find out what the last guy had charged so I could offer a better deal.

'Well,' I'd say, once I'd found the golden number, 'It's all eminently doable and there's no need to worry. My fee would probably be in the £250 range for this.'

'Really?' they'd say. 'Wow, that's excellent. Way less than the guy charged last year. Cuppa?'

Within a few months I was earning between £1600 and £2000 a month, and my financial worries were becoming a thing of the past. I got up-to-date on my mortgage payments and began the long process of paying off my credit cards. In the end, it took around two years to finally pay off my credit cards, and it was a glorious feeling to be finally debt free.

The driving ban eventually ran its course and what with not having to walk or take the bus everywhere, my productivity soared. It was a great time. I realised with quiet satisfaction that I did not need to worry about money anymore. I got a nice car. I was absurdly motivated, bringing in £25,000 to £30,000 a year.

It was taking its toll, however. I told myself I could work when it suited me, but because I really, really liked money, I was working all hours. The novelty soon wore thin. I was cash rich, but time poor. Not only that, but I would work for anyone and everyone, no matter who they were and where they were based, and this isn't always a good thing. Let me tell you a story about that.

The Trannies of Levenshulme

I remember very clearly my wake-up call – the day I realised I needed to get my business organised and move to the next level.

Mick had phoned. He was a van driver I did accounts for.

'Simon.'

'Mick.'

'Do you do computer people?' He meant 'do' their accounts.

'Of course.' I'd been specialising in 'computer people' accounting for a while. In those days I was of course a 'specialist' in everything.

'Right. You need to do a friend of mine, Graham. In a right mess, he is.'

I went that evening, around eight. It was my eleventh customer visit that day, back and forth across so-called Greater Manchester. All I'd eaten was a Ginsters pie, cheese and onion, at three that afternoon. It was all still very much down there, turning my stomach into an open-cast acid mine. My expensive new shoes had rubbed the bubble off a penny-sized blister just under my ankle bone.

And Levenshulme, I discovered, was not the most salubrious of districts. Limping past stacks of dog mess, I found the address. It was a shop in a dingy parade with its windows blacked out. Now, there were only two reasons I could think of for the windows to be blacked out. Either the shopkeeper was extremely photosensitive, or it was one of those places you went to ease life's burden with a 'massage'.

Either way, I needed the business.

I knocked and a nice-looking young woman let me in. She didn't look like a massage parlour hostess. She looked like she was in the middle of some housework. She said Graham was upstairs and to go on up. So I did. It was stuffy and kind of run down. At the landing I was met by a not-very-nice-looking older woman with big hair and blue eye shadow. She was wearing a lime-green, polyester pant-suit. There was something familiar about her.

'Simon.'

'Oh. Hi Mick.'

'Now you can see why my wife left me.'

'Erm. Yeah.'

'Graham's just in there.'

'Thanks.'

Graham, at least, was not dressed as a woman. He was sitting at a table covered with computer bits. But stacked in cages around three walls were at least 200 rats. We chatted about his accounts. I didn't actually count the rats. I was trying not to notice them. I'm not a huge fan of rats. I felt sure they were getting agitated, sniffing the air to get a bead on the growing patch of blood on my right sock. He asked if I wanted a coffee. I said I did. We chatted some more and then a maid brought coffee on a silver tray. A French maid, in a very short French maid's outfit. She was six foot two. She had ruby-red lips and a good, strong jaw line. Thick black hairs sprouted from her fishnet stockings. She had long blonde hair and five-o'clock shadow. She looked like Joey Ramone.

'Sugar, honey?' she said, her Adam's apple going up and down like the lifts on the Lloyds Building.

'No thanks,' I said.

It was Graham's girlfriend, Roma, who ran this 'facility' for transvestites (a great business idea, that. Clients could chill out, read a book, try on outfits, whatever, for £80 a day. More on great business ideas later).

I thought: I've got to get organised.

I sensed that I had hit a ceiling, that as a one-man-band there wasn't much more money I could make. And I wanted to make more. Much more. Exponentially more. Somebody, I can't remember who just now, put it like this: when you have a job, what you own is your time, and you sell it to the highest bidder. When you work for yourself what you own is your job, and that feels better, it's a step in the right direction, but it doesn't necessarily make you any richer. We are entrepreneurs, remember. There is only one option for us: owning a company. Because when you own a company you own the means of making wealth. It was that last step I wanted to make.

I had to get organised. Not long after doing the books for Graham, and for Roma, his girlfriend, I did.

Whorf! – The Big Idea

As these things go – life, that is – it didn't happen right away. First I found myself moving down south again. This was occasioned by two things. One, my girlfriend at the time, a brilliant young thing who slogged through law school and articling and all that difficult, time-consuming rigmarole, had landed a job with a top firm in London (last I heard she was teaching scuba diving in New Zealand. See?).

Two, I'd had my fill of drab, rainy Manchester. This was just before the felicitous bombing of 1996 sparked all the regeneration. So I moved to Hemel Hempstead, only because my parents had landed in the area when they'd left Manchester, and I knew it vaguely and it seemed OK.

Financially I was in a good position to move, having got my mortgage back on track and paid off my credit cards. I decided not to sell my house, but to rent it out instead, and sorted myself some rented accommodation down south which meant I didn't have any big financial commitments when I moved.

I was starting from scratch again but that didn't bother me. I thought I'd be able to just replicate what I'd done in Manchester. But for some reason the fish weren't nearly as biting in this pond. I was sort of bumbling along with a sub-optimum mixed bag of clients when my next big idea came along. In boxing terms, my first idea, the 'year-end-for-£99-and-book-keeping-for-£10-a-month idea', could be described as the probing left jab. What came next was the knockout right hook.

This analysis, of course, would emerge in hindsight. It didn't feel like I was having a 'knockout right hook' moment at the time. It did feel like something, though. I think it was a *whorf* moment, a mini one.

I will explain the whorf. It starts as a little idea, a brief whiff of opportunity. Something you've never actually articulated before, but when you do it seems so obvious and the Universe of Possibilities starts rushing outward in all directions like in the instant after the Big Bang.

It all starts as a niggling problem. Here's an example. A bit far-fetched, but work with me. Your dad's birthday's coming up and you have absolutely no idea what to get him. Then you have this little thought: 'Hey, I could make him a birthday card with a funny message, myself, using that software that came with the computer.' Maybe a friend did it for you once. Anyway you start messing around with the software, and it's actually really fun. Then you start fooling around with ideas for your dad's card, experimenting with photographs, or maybe a little free drawing, which entails getting to know the software better, and all that is really fun.

Then comes this flash of an idea: you could make a unique and funny card for your wife's birthday too, which is coming up next month. You could do cards for *all* your friends! They'll love them! (Though not nearly as much as you'll love doing them). But then you start running low on ideas so you begin to pay attention to greeting cards in shops, analysing the ones you like. You look on the web, maybe go to some arty card shops and galleries, and all that is really fun. Then, of course, you are floored, you are totally flattened, with the most stupendous idea of all: you could go into business with a line of cards all on your own! You could make money at this! You start talking to people. There's a cousin in Congleton who has a graphic design business and you call him up and he tells you loads and doesn't seem to remember what a prick you were as a kid. You start reading up on the greeting card business. You're totally consumed.

Have you ever been through a *whorf* like this? It's a word I made up and would like to introduce into the English language, please, Mr Solemn Bearded Guys sitting in robes around the long obsidian table who decide these things. Whorf! It's a cross between 'Whoosh' and 'Morph' ('Moorsh' doesn't sound right) and captures that flume-ride where, in this case, what started as the niggling problem of what to get Dad for his birthday becomes, in 72 hours, a whole new dazzling future.

Whorfs are not always good for family life. To your wife and kids you become useless. They're all excited about a summer holiday, say, and all you can think about is cards. They try and tell you something that is troubling them and you start giggling because you've thought of a great gag – for a card. Then you say sorry and nod and say 'Uh huh,' but you're really agonising over what weight of card would be best. You gasp with relief when they all go out Friday evening and you sprint up the stairs and fool around with ideas, but then the front door slams what seems like five minutes later and they call up, 'We're home!', and you curse and hop around in fury.

Anyway, my little whorf came on a September morning in 1996. My niggling problem was how to get the business going again. I had serious money to make. Then I remembered something. It just came into my head. Something small but important. My Messing Around phase was starting to dish up tasty tidbits. Back at Uppal and Warr, quite an important group of clients were IT contractors, a species which were at that time threatening to overrun the earth.

These guys were legally obliged to do things like file accounts with Companies House and do corporate tax returns and VAT returns and payroll and all sorts of incomprehensible mumbo jumbo which, if you didn't do it absolutely correctly, to the last jot and tittle, would land you in a festering Thai prison for the next 60 years. Or at least that's how it felt to these guys. There were companies around who would relieve you of the terrible burden for £50 or £60 a month. We used to do it at Uppal and Warr for £50 or £60 a month. My little idea was that I would do it for £30 a month.

Yessiree. My oh my. *Whorf!*

I got the number for *Computer Contractor* magazine and found out how much a decent classified ad would cost and how many words I could cram into it. Then I cleared the kitchen table and began composing the ad. It really flowed. I knew the language. All the stuff I could do for those hard-pressed IT contractors! But when I got to the bit about me, about the company, I felt funny. The ad packed all the punch of an established, quietly-confident international corporation, and yet the phone number looked distinctly naked, somehow. Regional. Dial those eleven digits and for sure a phone would ring in some bloke's kitchen. And the address: 1 Bluebell Close, Chaulden Vale, Hemel Hempstead... Bluebell Close? Not a bad address if you run a cottage industry in wild berry preserves or illustrate children's books about fluffy woodland creatures. But this was serious business, top-shelf stuff.

I drummed my fingers. I drummed and I drummed, expectantly now, because I could already feel my Messing Around server whirring and chunking. There was a way around this, and... yes... there it was. I picked up the phone and got the number for Regus Offices. They did virtual business premises (started by Mark Dixon, my kind of guy – left school at 16, made his first £800,000 selling his burger van business). For a fee you could get a postal address, phone number and even a meeting room. An hour later I had a head office at 10 Stratton Street, Mayfair, and when anybody dialled the central London number, at exactly one-third the way through the second ring, the low voice of an audibly ravishing woman would intone suggestively:

'SJD Accountancy...?'

And that was just head office. SJD Accountancy was now everywhere – Aberdeen, Bath, Coventry, Derby – I just worked my way down the alphabet. It wasn't cheap, but it was worth it. In the week my ad appeared, I had eight calls. Same thing the week after, and the week after. That's when I knew I was on to something big.

I was 27.

I had wasted so much time.

CHAPTER FIVE

How I Turned £30K into £75 Million

There's a big difference between £30k and £75 million – so how did I turn a successful £30k-a-year business into a multi-million-pound operation? Millionaires often leave out this crucial detail when talking through the story of their success. I've read plenty of business autobiographies and lost count of the number of times an author goes into great detail about humble beginnings and then, whoosh! Suddenly, he or she is earning millions and the reader thinks: 'How did that happen?' In Eddy Stobart's autobiography, for example, he goes from owning two lorries to 1000 lorries. How did that happen?

As a matter of fact, there's a good reason millionaires don't detail their rise from thousands to millions. It's because the story is boring. Businesses grow little by little, year by year. There's nothing glamorous or exciting about that. 'Overnight' success stories are hardly ever *real* overnight success stories. Most millionaires grow their fortune bit by bit.

However, there is a crucial 'secret' to turning mini-bucks into mega-bucks. That secret is duplication. Duplication is how business empires grow. All the big guns like Starbucks and McDonald's started with just one business. And then they opened another. And another. After many years and lots of patience, they became 'overnight successes', with branches all over the world.

Once I had a successful business up and running, I realised I needed to duplicate it. That way I could also duplicate my income. So, at one stage I was earning £30k a year. When I duplicated my business, I roughly doubled my income. The more

I duplicated the business, the more I earned, until eventually I was earning millions.

I'm making it sound very simple. That's because it is. But there are a few potentially sticky moments in the process, so let's talk in more detail about exactly how I duplicated my business.

Stage One: Getting Staff to Help

When you start a business, you generally do everything yourself. In my first few years, I licked stamps, answered phone calls, bought stationery and carried out a whole host of other minor tasks that took my time and attention away from the most important thing – winning new clients. Now, there's nothing wrong with that. It's what you need to do when you start out, unless you want to get a risky bank loan or remortgage your house so you can hire staff straight away.

The problem is, most people get stuck in the 'doing everything' stage. They don't realise they need to move away from doing everything themselves and get help.

When my business was turning a nice, consistent profit each year, I realised I needed someone to do all the stamp-licking sorts of tasks. This, I decided, would free me up to win even more clients.

Hiring stamp-licking staff is usually quite easy. I say *usually* easy, because it can go wrong. At one stage, I hired a receptionist called Jo who made Jo Brand look cheerful (I'll tell you more about her later). But generally, it's easy to find someone young and enthusiastic who is capable of licking stamps and doing other general admin tasks. As it happened, in the early days I got very lucky and hired a bright 18-year-old who still works for me today. She's now one of my best regional managers.

So, *finding* my first staff member was easy, but there was a catch. I was earning a very comfortable £30k a year, but my admin person was costing me £14k a year. That was nearly half my wages. Ouch. And to make matters worse, I had to spend time training the admin person (so I didn't have all that much extra time to visit clients in the beginning) *and* it was some time before I saw the profits from any new clients I brought in.

I decided to be patient and look at things in the long-term. Yes, my income would drop, but I was confident the business would eventually be more profitable. After I'd trained my staff member and freed up some time, I was able to grow the business even more. So yes, it did work. Hiring an admin person (eventually) made me more money. That's stage one.

Stage Two: Building the Business

Once you've got more free time, you need to continue building up the business. This means long hours. While I was building up my business, nothing was too much trouble and no distance too far to travel for a potential client. I frequently worked 15 to 18 hour days. I flew to Scotland from London on many occasions (a 12-hour round trip by the time the airport commutes were built in) just to see one potential client, and sometimes they wouldn't even show up! This never detracted me from getting that one extra client.

Of course, this was easy hard work. It was a labour of love. Stage three is where things got tougher…

Stage Three: Duplicating Yourself

This is where things can get sticky. Not because duplicating yourself is difficult, but because it means trusting someone else to do your job and handle your clients. It involves a big leap of faith. Courage. When I duplicated myself, it meant stepping away from the business and realising it was something in its own right. And of course, it also meant trusting someone else to do my job and make money for me.

Once I'd made up my mind to find a 'duplicate me', it

actually wasn't all that hard to let go. I just had to find the right person and let them get on with things. In some ways I was lucky. The first 'duplicate me' I hired happened to be very good, trustworthy, reliable and did a great job. If I'd hired someone awful who'd stolen my clients or handled the business badly and lost me money, who knows? Maybe I'd never have gotten past the £30k stage.

Probably, quite a few potential millionaires have been thwarted by hiring the wrong person in the early stages, and thought: 'Well, I just can't trust anyone else to run things – I'll have to carry on doing it all myself.' So watch out for that one. If you hire the wrong person, don't give up. Try again.

I'm probably the world's worst trainer and have very little patience when it comes to teaching others, so my basic technique was to hire people who could figure things out for themselves. This seemed to work out rather well. People who are naturally motivated will do very well for your business.

Of course, it did mean a few people fell by the wayside. I can't really be bothered with anyone who can't figure things out for themselves so an employee who couldn't work things out fast had to go. And the truth is, if you take a 'hands off' approach, sometimes people take advantage of you.

I remember in the early days, I hired an accountant called Peter who typed furiously on his PC all day long. I was rather pleased I'd hired someone so hardworking, but then Peter went on holiday and we received word from clients that he hadn't been doing his job properly.

A quick look on his PC showed that all his furious typing had been on MSN. We knew this because he'd rather stupidly saved an 11-page manuscript of his outpourings to a girl he'd fallen in love with online on his computer (I say girl – she could have been an eighty-year-old man for all anyone, including Peter, knew).

If I had my time again, I'd definitely manage people more closely. But you can also have the opposite problem when hiring a 'duplicate you'. It can be very difficult to stop yourself looking over their shoulder at first. It took me a little while to realise that other people didn't do things exactly how I'd have done them, and I learned to bite my tongue. You can't stifle people. You have to let them do things their way, and who knows – they might even do the job better than you.

You also have to get your 'duplicate you' really passionate about your business, and onboard with the great products/services you provide. You can hire the best person in the world, but if you don't make sure they care about the job, chances are they'll be de-motivated. So it's important to share your business passion with staff.

I found my first 'duplicate me' at a recruitment agency, but there really are dozens of ways of finding good employees. Social media sites are good, as are fixed-fee recruitment websites. Or you could always put an advert in the newspaper. There's no magic formula here. Just use your common sense and take a leap of faith, and if it all goes wrong, just hire someone else and try again.

Stage Four: Duplicating the Business

What's the difference between a small business and a multi-million pound company? Multiple outlets. McDonald's has lots of restaurants, Starbucks has lots of cafés and my accounting company reaps profits from branches all over the UK.

Duplication is a very common story in business. As I said earlier, I was basically 'borrowing' ideas from entrepreneurs who had succeeded before me. Create one successful business and multiply it by 100. Or 1,000. That's how businesses go from small fry to big potatoes.

Take McDonald's for example. When McDonald's began back in the 1940s, it was just one, stand-alone hamburger restaurant. What made it special was a very clever 'speedee service system' that meant customers got their food in double-quick time. The brothers who founded the restaurant, Richard and Maurice McDonald, decided that instead of giving customers a choice of toppings, every burger would come with the same toppings: mustard, ketchup, onion and gherkin. This, among other things, made the service 'speedee'.

The restaurant did very well. But it wasn't making millions. For that to happen, the restaurant had to be duplicated. Along came a man called Ray Kroc, who opened a franchised McDonald's restaurant in Illinois. And then another restaurant was opened and another. Decades passed, and then one day the McDonald's company was earning millions.

In 2009, McDonald's had 31,000 restaurants worldwide, each earning a net income of around about $30k each quarter. That's only £20-25k per restaurant. Not mega-bucks. But combine the income of each restaurant, and you have a quarterly net income of $979.5 million.

The Starbucks story is similar. In 1971, Starbucks was a lonely coffee bean shop in Seattle, the only brain-child of coffee connoisseurs Jerry Baldwin, Zev Siegl and Gordon Bowker. In its first six years, Starbucks modestly traded darkly roasted coffee beans and coffee equipment designed for the perfect home brew. But the company was soon to take on a new life after a chance encounter with coffee enthusiast Harold Schultz.

Schultz had big plans for the small company. He wanted to create a coffee shop that was a 'home from home' for customers. A cosy, friendly environment where they could enjoy the darkly roasted coffee he loved so much. So in 1986 he opened a coffee shop. It did very well. So he opened another. And another. Skip to 23 years later.

In 2009, Starbucks owned 16,709 coffee shops worldwide, and each shop earned, on average, a net income of around $25,000 in that year. Again, not a staggeringly huge amount. But multiply that by 16,709 and you have a very favourable profit of $390.8 million.

McDonald's and Starbucks make millions because they have many different outlets all over the world. Each outlet makes a modest profit, but the combined profits from *every* outlet amounts to millions.

So to truly make money, the secret is to have more than one office/shop/location. Once I put in all the hard work and learned how to duplicate myself, I realised I needed to duplicate the business.

I'd love to say I wanted to make the world a better place with my fleet of accountancy businesses, but the truth is my main goal was to make more money. I realised if I opened another office in Scotland and it won more clients, then I'd increase my profits. So that's what I did.

Now here's the thing. Opening a duplicate business is a bit like starting a new business. Things are slow at first. The profits don't come flying in immediately and in the early stages I was only winning a few new clients with my second business. You don't go from having one business to 50 profitable ones overnight.

Luckily I was realistic. I'd done the sums and I reasoned that *some* extra profit was OK. It didn't have to be lots at first. So I was happy for the second business to tick over and build up gradually.

Then I started opening more branches. I realised that the business was working in London, so why not try it out in Manchester, Liverpool and even further afield?

I wrote a manual that outlined the great service the company should offer, and gave rough guidelines for new managers to follow, then offered good incentives so managers would treat the business like their own and work hard to reap rewards. I knew I had to make these businesses as independent as possible and step back. This meant letting the new manager take the helm.

Every 'new' business is different, even if it's a duplication, so I also let myself learn from each new venture and didn't expect too much too soon. Crucially, I also didn't spend a fortune on duplicating the business just because I could.

Stage Five: Turn Negatives into Positives

When everything is up and running, there will be the occasional bad day. These days are opportunities to turn negatives into positives. After a number of good business years, a new piece of government legislation was passed (called IR35) that threatened to have a seriously negative effect on my business.

I worried about this. There were many staff working under me and I had lots of financial responsibilities. I had a few bad weeks. Then I decided to become an expert in IR35 and turn this negative into an advantage. I became the person who knew all about this piece of legislation and won more customers as a result. Ultimately, this meant the business did better than before.

McDonald's hit a huge problem when the film 'Supersize Me' was released in 2004, which depicted a healthy thirty-something man eating McDonald's morning, noon and night and suffering some rather major health consequences as a result. The public began thinking twice about eating McDonald's. Profits fell. So the company decided to get, OK not healthy, but healthier. They started selling carrot sticks with their burgers and buying organic milk. They copied Starbucks and sold posh coffee in big paper cups. Profits grew again.

Your business and the market in which you operate will change over time. Changes that at first appear negative can be made into positives. So make sure you make the most of the changes and your business will continue to thrive.

Give Yourself Time

Duplicating yourself and your business takes time, so don't expect everything to happen overnight. In my case, it took some 14 years to turn one client into 10,000 clients. I had 80 clients in year one, 150 by the end of year two and 300 by the end of year three, and things continued to snowball until eventually I had over 10,000 all over the UK. McDonald's took around 40 years to become a global success story and Starbucks around 20.

There is a saying that goes something like: 'Most people massively overestimate what they can achieve in a year, and massively underestimate what they can achieve in a decade.' This is particularly true when building a business. So it will take time and hard work (easy hard work), but ultimately if you keep on duplicating a successful business formula, profits will follow.

So that's it. My life from schoolboy to millionaire. If you think this chapter seems a bit on the short side, you're right. There really isn't much to say about how I transformed a £30k business into a multi-million-pound one. I just duplicated the same successful concept over and over again.

Now I want to tell you how *you* can start your own business and earn millions. Ready to find out? Let's get started.

PART 2

Why Avoiding University Makes You Rich and Famous

CHAPTER SIX

Those Who Made It Without a Degree

I'm now going to share with you the inspiring stories of UK multimillionaires and billionaires who made it without a degree. In fact, many of these entrepreneurs amassed their fortunes without gaining any academic qualifications.

University is fine. It's great, even. Universities teach useful and powerful things. If my child has to go to a specialist doctor, I really want that doctor to have gone to a great university. When I'm flying somewhere, I fervently hope the men and women who designed the plane got put through their paces – at university. I'm glad you need a degree in structural engineering in this country if you're going to design a bridge or a skyscraper. And if I ever need a lawyer to represent me or my family in some crucial case, I hope that lawyer came top of the class in a really tough degree course.

University is great. But not for everybody.

I said before that I believe the academic treadmill is actually harmful to the entrepreneurial drive. I stand by that. For one thing it gives you the false sense that you know a lot of stuff, when you don't. You may know *about* a lot of stuff, but in terms of actual skills based on experience, in terms of real, how-to knowledge that leads to confident action, you know nothing.

For another thing, it fosters the mindset of dependency. Unless you've been in the grubby world of commerce and mucked in with the actual creation of products or services and caused money to change hands as a result, or failed to, business will remain a dark mystery and you'll come to believe that it's only freaks and demons who get involved at such a low level. You'll wait around for a safe, comfortable position to open up in a corporation or the government. In short, the academic treadmill ingrains a tolerance for tedium, a reverence for hoop-jumping and the habit of thinking small.

The wildly successful entrepreneurs I'm going to talk about in this section all left the education system as soon as they could – often without any qualifications at all. University was certainly not on their agenda. You'll have heard of some of them and you may think, 'Sure, they're the famous ones, the exceptions.' But wait. Read their stories. They weren't famous or exceptional when they started out, or even when they made their respective killer moves. They were on the ground, mucking in, doing what seemed natural. *Then* they got rich and famous.

They're all over 50, but that doesn't mean their experiences aren't relevant today. If anything, the climate is even riper nowadays for quality, enterprising people. I hope you find these stories as inspiring as I do.

Sir Richard Branson, born 1950
Billionaire founder and owner of the Virgin group
Education: Left school at 16 with one O level

Who hasn't heard of Richard Branson? With his daring lifestyle and charitable activities, Branson is probably one of the highest profile billionaires around. A real breath of fresh air in the business world, Branson challenges the view that rich men are suit-wearing fuddy duddies and enjoys an enviably luxurious lifestyle.

Born in Blackheath, South London, Branson wasn't from humble beginnings – but that doesn't matter. What matters is that he left the education system as soon as he could and Got On With It. His dad was a barrister, his granddad was a High Court judge and a Privy Councillor and Branson himself attended a posh private school. However, Branson was mildly dyslexic and rubbish at school, so decided to quit at the first opportunity – a decision that catapulted him straight into business success.

Messing Around

Branson actually did very little messing around, in the sense of doing rubbish jobs and learning about the real world. He pretty much went into business straight away, and in fact started two businesses at school, one growing Christmas trees and another one raising budgerigars.

Neither made his fortune, but they certainly gave him a flavour of how business works.

The Business

When he left school at 16, Branson began his first successful business, *Student* magazine. In an interview with CNN he said he didn't do it to make money, but because he thought the way he was taught was stupid and he fancied editing a magazine so he could have the editorial platform to say so. He didn't even realise what a great business idea it was. Students were a valued target audience for advertisers, but there was no national student magazine at the time (hmmm… is there one now?). He went around flogging ad space himself for his first edition and sold £8,000 worth. This was in 1966! He printed 50,000 copies and didn't even have to charge for the magazine because his costs were covered.

Next, he began buying up crates of 'cut-out' records and selling them out of his car boot to shops. Cut-outs were copies of LPs which record companies felt they couldn't sell through the usual channels, for whatever reason, so they'd snip off a corner of the cover and pile them up for the bargain bin. Then Branson started selling these cut-outs by mail-order.

In his early twenties, Branson and a friend, Nik Powell, opened a record shop in Notting Hill Gate, London, called Virgin Records and Tapes, specialising in experimental rock and pop from Germany (known as 'Krautrock'). They called the shop 'Virgin', according to Branson, because they were so wet behind the ears when it came to business.

Bumps on the Road

Virgin Records did well, but Branson and Powell weren't exactly running everything the way they should, and were quickly fined tens of thousands of pounds for tax evasion. This was a massive bump in the road, but, as is often the way with entrepreneurialism, the 'bump' led to greater things. To pay the tax fine, Branson and Powell stepped up a gear and expanded their chain of shops.

The Big Business

As Virgin shops became more successful, Branson and Powell

launched an actual record label, Virgin Records. By this stage, Branson had earned enough money to buy a big house in the country, in which he installed a recording studio, leasing it out to new artists.

In a staggering stroke of good fortune, Branson's first signing was multi-instrumentalist, Mike Oldfield, whose *Tubular Bells* album sold five-million copies. The label grew quickly to become one of the top six record companies in the world, boasting household names, including Belinda Carlisle, Genesis, Phil Collins, Simple Minds, Janet Jackson and The Rolling Stones. The equity of Virgin Music Group was sold to EMI in 1992 in a billion-dollar deal.

After that, Branson went off and launched businesses in, well, everything. The Virgin brand has since expanded into air and rail travel, mobile phones, finance, weddings, retail, drinks, hotels and gymnasiums, with around 200 companies in over 30 countries employing more than 25,000 people.

Branson just can't stop thinking up new stuff. His next venture will be Virgin Fuels, which he claims will offer cheaper fuel for cars and planes. He has also pledged to invest the profits of Virgin Atlantic and Virgin Trains into research for environmentally friendly fuels.

A great innovator, Branson is the first entrepreneur to offer space travel, at the bargain price of $200,000, and Virgin Galactic is currently taking bookings for flights into space. Granted, the technology isn't quite ready yet, but ticket holders are offered a speculative space flight sometime in the future. He has also set up a new Global science and technology prize—The Virgin Earth Challenge—which will award $25 million for a commercially viable design which will result in the net removal of greenhouse gases each year for at least ten years.

Life without Qualifications

Branson is well-known for his derring-do, and keeps his fabulous wealth from becoming dull by regularly putting his life at risk. In 1985, he set out from New York to beat the record for crossing the Atlantic by boat, but had to be rescued after his boat sank. It did not deter him. In 1986, he beat the record by two hours. A year later, his hot-air balloon, 'Virgin Atlantic Flyer', was the first hot-air balloon to cross the Atlantic, but this was after several, very dangerous failed flights.

A family man, Branson enjoys spending time at home with his wife and children, and uses a sizable portion of his wealth to try and make the world a better place. Without a degree or any higher education, Branson has managed to become both wealthy and a fine, upstanding citizen. Now there's a thing.

Sir Philip Green, born 1952
Britain's richest self-made billionaire
Education: Left school at 15 without any formal qualifications

When Philip Green left school at 15, little did his teachers know he'd go on to become one of the UK's most successful businessmen. Listed sixth on the *Sunday Times* rich list in 2009, Green's wealth was only topped in the UK by the Duke of Westminster (who inherited his swag from the Grosvenor clan) and several foreign billionaires like Chelsea FC's owner, Roman Abramovich. For a man with no formal qualifications, Sir Philip hasn't done too badly.

Green was born in 1952 in Croydon, South London, to a normal working-class family, but one with a good handle on running businesses. Between then, his parents ran garages and electrical shops, and managed property, and a young Green helped out at weekends. By the time he was 15, he decided he didn't see the point of school and quit without any qualifications, preferring to take his education in the real world.

Messing Around

From a young age, Green changed oil and wiped windscreens at his parents' garages, but when he quit school he wasn't interested in working for the family business. Instead, he got a full-time Messing Around job. It was a fantastically educational one, working for a company that imported shoes from the Far East. Wholesale, in other words.

For four years, Green was a shoe slave, filing, working in the warehouse and running errands for the big dudes, otherwise known as the salesmen. Then – only then, mind – he was promoted to a sales job. As a salesman he got to know all the shoe retailers and how they did business, plus received a golden education in Hong Kong and Taiwanese manufacturing.

The Business

At the age of 23, Green decided to take the plunge. He took himself off to Hong Kong with a view to importing something to sell himself, and decided to invest in, not shoes, but jeans. This was in 1975, when every hippy owned a pair of jeans, and Green knew a profitable fashion trend when he saw one. So he got a £20,000 loan from the bank (I don't want you to borrow money to start your business, but this is what Philip did) and started importing jeans.

Selling jeans went pretty well – so well, in fact, that by 1979 Green was able to make the big move. He heard of a small chain of ten designer clothes outlets that had gone into receivership. The entire stock, worth £35k, retail, was up for grabs. So he grabbed it, sight unseen. And when he did see the stuff, it wasn't so bad.

Knowing the value of presentation, Green had the clothes dry-cleaned, put on satin hangers and wrapped in polythene. Then, rather than just mark it up a few pounds, he decided to go into retail himself. He bought a shop on London's fashionable Conduit Street from a guy he knew who was retiring, and started flogging his haul.

In 1981 (now aged 29) he bought a shop on Bond Street. In interviews he says he walked into the shop on a Friday afternoon, offered £75k without even seeing the stock and exchanged contracts the following Monday.

The Big Business

Before Green had even redecorated, he had a guy on the phone wanting to buy the shop. This guy was very persistent. Green said OK, £250k. Deal! But Green wasn't quite finished with the shop he'd just bought. He told the guy that he couldn't have the shop for six weeks. That's because he really liked the stock, which was quality leather stuff. He asked the guy he'd bought the shop from if there was any more of this good stock anywhere. Yes, said the guy – stacks of it over in Milan. So Green went to Milan, bought four or five container loads and spent the next six weeks flogging leather. And everybody liked it. There were queues snaking down Bond Street.

Green went on to buy a failing chain of shops for a bargain price, and used his business sense to create a successful retail business. To stock the shops, he went to Paris armed with three suitcases and stocked up on beautiful, designer gear. Then he went to Hong Kong and asked the manufacturers there to copy it. He restocked the UK shops, retooled, got credit flowing again and had the business breaking even in four months.

In 1985, a buyer offered Green £7 million for his flourishing retail business and Green accepted. After settling everything up, he walked away with around £3.5 million – at the age of 32.

Bumps on the Road

Most entrepreneurs experience a few bumps on the road while they're amassing their fortune, but Green seems to have been blessed with lots of luck and a smooth road to travel along. I don't want you to worry about that. I'm sure he must have had some bumps on the road that he doesn't talk about, but the truth is his business CV reads like a man with the Midas touch – success after success, and always acquiring more money. He even managed to turn around the fortunes of failing British Home Stores in the 1990s, tripling its profits within a year.

The Big Business

In 2002, Green bought the Arcadia Group, which includes Burton, Dorothy Perkins, Evans, Miss Selfridge, Outfit, Topshop/Topman and Wallis. It has been another huge success story. On the 20th of October 2005, Green awarded Arcadia shareholders a £1.3 billion dividend. As joint owners of 92 per cent of the group, he received £1.17 billion – the largest payout to an individual in British corporate history.

Life without Qualifications

Green's story is all about know-how, guts, vision and luck. It's not about degrees, training courses and qualifications. OK, so luck is just, well, lucky, but Green's guts and vision didn't come from higher education. They came from time spent in the real world, mucking in and learning how business works.

Green now enjoys a fabulous billionaire lifestyle, as you might expect, but his love of business means he's not yet ready to retire. I imagine we'll hear many more of his success stories before his time in business is through.

Stephen Marks, born 1946
Multimillionaire founder and owner of FCUK
Education: Left school at 16 to play tennis

Stephen Marks is the man who made it socially acceptable to walk around with a bag saying 'FCUK the Sale' written on it – and he made a lot of money doing so. Now a multimillionaire, Marks is generally regarded as one of the UK's most successful fashion bosses and the FCUK clothing chain continues to add to his millions.

Born in 1946 in Harrow, Marks spent much of his childhood helping out in his father's hairdressing salon. Both his parents were hairdressers, and Marks's background was a humble one – albeit tinged with greatness. A brilliant, young tennis player, he was tipped to be a potential Wimbledon champ and left secondary modern school at 16 to pursue this ambition.

Messing Around

After a brief mess around with tennis, Marks realised he lacked the dedication to become a professional player and that was the end of that. He realised he had to get a proper job (more Messing Around) and began sweeping floors and delivering coats for Leonard Sheraton's – one of the big women's clothing chains at the time.

After six years of messing around at Sheraton's, quietly absorbing useful business lessons such as stock control along the way, Marks worked for the *haute couture* label, Louis Feraud.

The Business

Working as an underling soon got too much, and Marks decided to design his first fashion range – elegant suits for women under the 'Stephen Marks' label. Moderate success followed.

Then a stroke of luck. Marks happened to get chatting to a Paris fashion designer, Pierre D'Alby, and this fine, French fashion fellow persuaded Marks that he should launch his own clothing range. Marks thought this sounded like a good idea and decided to call it French Collection. Then he had a rethink, and changed it to French Connection after seeing the 1971 gangster film of the same name. With typical verve, he launched his stores in posh places like Sloane Square.

Bumps on the Road

French Connection expanded to America, but at the end of the 80s it was struggling. Marks had taken a back seat and his eye off the ball, but now he came galloping back to the rescue. Fortunately, he had some spare cash. As one of the backers of the Hard Rock restaurant chain, he'd got a large slice of the £300 million windfall when it was sold to Rank.

The Big Business

In 1997, the moment came for which Marks will always be remembered. Marks asked ad guru Trevor Beattie to dream up an advertising campaign. Beattie spotted that the company faxes to the Hong Kong office were labelled 'FCUK'.

Bingo!

Where could you not go with this? 'Hot as FCUK', 'mile high FCUK', and 'cool as FCUK', etc. It titillated so many kids that profits trebled. In 2001, French Connection hit San Francisco with big banners on the new store saying: 'San Francisco's first FCUK'.

The media attention the company got, thanks to protests from the Church of England (among others) and an investigation by the Advertising Standards Authority, was priceless.

Life without Qualifications

Now Marks continues to tinker around with his multimillion chain, making sure it stays profitable, but he has plenty of time for his tennis hobby, his family and generally the things in life that are fun.

Despite never taking further education, Marks seems to be a pleasant and well-rounded fellow – not to mention very rich. He puts a whole load of his money towards training up young British tennis players, and uses his wealth to try and open up the game for everyone and remove the snobbery and elitism that has dogged tennis for years.

John Bloor, born 1944
Multimillionaire property investor and owner of Triumph
Motorcycles
Education: Left school at 15 without any formal qualifications,
after barely six months in secondary education

Multimillionaire John Bloor created one of the UK's largest privately-owned house-building companies, but he is best known for reviving much loved British brand, Triumph Motorcycles. And would you believe he barely spent six months at secondary school and left with no qualifications?

The son of a Derbyshire miner, John Bloor was a sickly teenager so spent lots of time off school, and packed it in entirely when he was 15.

Messing Around

Before his 16th birthday, Bloor joined a local building contractor as a trainee plasterer. He chose to mess around with something that actually was messy – plaster is sticky stuff. He got covered in it for two years. Then he set up his own business and, rather amazingly, built his own house by the age of 20. So he had his own home and his own business at an age when many young people today are still in full-time education.

The Business

Bloor was clever. He got into a very profitable industry – property – early on, and his construction business, Bloor Homes, continued to grow and grow. Bloor stuck at it, and after 40 years Bloor Homes became one of the UK's largest privately-owned house-building companies. That's why he's so rich, but it's a boring story compared to the motorcycles.

The Big Business

OK, so technically Bloor Homes is Bloor's 'big business'. But the real 'big business', the one where Bloor's heart and soul lies, is Triumph Motorcycles.

Motorcycles? That's right. John Bloor single-handedly revived UK motorcycle manufacturing, transforming it from a cottage industry into a major export manufacturer.

Once an iconic British brand, Triumph Motorcycles died a death in the early 1980s, thanks to competition from the Far East. Bloor found this heartbreaking. Steve McQueen rode a Triumph motorcycle in *The Great Escape*, as did Marlon Brando in *The Wild One*. For years, it was as cool as a Harley Davidson. But by 1983 those days were long gone. Cash had run out and the factory in Meriden closed its doors. Liquidation and the sale of assets followed. The site was bulldozed.

Bloor was sad. He loved Triumph and wanted the UK to keep on manufacturing motorcycles. But first and foremost, he was a property developer. It just so happened that that the Triumph factory site was being auctioned off for development, and as a canny constructor Bloor checked out its property building potential. Honest. That's why he was there. But something mysterious happened to him while he was standing among the other greedy, insensitive developers. By God, he thought, I will save Triumph! Whorf! Then and there he *bought* the Triumph marque and rights! From the receiver!

To keep Triumph production going, Bloor licensed Les Harris, a motorbike fanatic who manufactured classic bike parts down in Devon, to carry on building the venerable 'Bonneville' – Triumph's flagship model since 1959. And for the next few years Les Harris and his small crew built Bonnevilles. It was hardly mass production. At peak they could do 14 a week. But it kept the Triumph brand ticking over while Bloor got his act together to re-launch Triumph once again onto the world stage.

After a few years, Bloor invested more than £80 million in rebuilding the marque and, in 1991, he opened the new Hinckley factory with state-of-the-art tooling. The re-launch was a big success and Triumph now produces over 45,000 motorcycles a year.

Bumps on the Road

Even multimillionaires have their off days, and Bloor has indeed had a few. There was a bit of a hiccup in 2002 when one of his new Triumph factories burned down, costing Bloor £4.5 million and stopping production for six months. But he used the downtime to improve production and Triumph is now one of the most efficient motorcycle builders in the world.

Also, after the 2008 credit crunch and subsequent 'tough economic times' in the UK, Bloor's property fortune plummeted. The 'clever' decision to run a property business didn't seem so clever when property prices fell, and Bloor lost hundreds of millions of pounds in just one year. Ouch. But despite a massive loss of profits, Bloor is still one of the wealthiest men in the UK and remains a shrewd businessman and profit-making property giant.

Life without Qualifications

Bloor has the proud title of being one of the richest men to hail from the Midlands. But an even better claim to fame is that he single-handedly saved Triumph from ruin and turned it into a profitable business that today makes millions. He's made a fortune doing something he really loves, and despite his lack of education he is a multimillionaire that British industry can be proud of.

Eddie and Malcolm Healey,
born circa 1938 and 1945 respectively
Achieved fabulous wealth from kitchens and property –
Malcolm is worth £600 million and brother Eddie
is worth £750 million
Education: Both left school at 16 without any formal
qualifications

Billionaires, Eddie and Malcolm Healey, were ranked 27th in the 2009 *Sunday Times* rich list, and guess what? They don't have an O level between them, let alone a degree. The Healey brothers keep out of the public eye, but their combined fortune of £1,350 million is worth more than old what's-his-name Richard Branson and the famous Barclay brothers.

Hailing from Hull in East Yorkshire, both Eddie and Malcolm left school at the age of 16 without any qualifications, and threw themselves straight into the real world of work.

Messing Around

After leaving school the brothers messed around, working in their father's painting and decorating business called Stanley's. They didn't like the paint fumes, though, so they joined their older brother, John, who ran another business, Status Discount. (Nepotistic messing around is fine.)

John's business did very well, and many years later was sold to MFI for £30 million in 1980. But a mere eight-digit fortune wasn't enough for Eddie and Malcolm. They set up their own businesses while John amassed his 'meagre' £30 million.

The Big Business

With a business education from their high-flying older brother,

Malcolm and Eddie didn't start small, oh no no no. They went straight into big business, setting up ambitious enterprises that netted both of them millions within a very short space of time.

In 1976, Malcolm set up Humber Kitchens, which began by supplying materials to the Healey family's stores. Later, he acquired the Hygena name, which he sold to MFI for £200 million in 1987, then went to the US, where he made a further £800 million from a similar operation.

Eddie's entrepreneurial drive also got into gear in the mid-1970s. By the 1980s, he was only interested in multimillion-pound developments. Banking on the money-making potential of out-of-town, disused industrial sites, he began building Retail World, in 1985, on an old steelworks site in Rotherham, South Yorkshire. He promised local councillors he would create the biggest shopping mall in Europe.

Bumps on the Road

Eddie's ambitious project ran into problems. Only a quarter of his planned £100 million development had been completed when the anchor store, Marks & Spencer, pulled out. Meanwhile, in nearby Sheffield, another Yorkshire developer, Paul Sykes, was having trouble raising finance for his rival Meadowhall project. Potential backers were spooked by the proximity of Healey's Retail World.

It was like two circuses converging on the same town on the same evening.

Eddie saw that it was either fight or fraternise. Fighting could kill off both ventures so, in 1987, he made a now famous phone call to Sykes proposing that they join forces. Sykes agreed, on the condition that Eddie scrap his world-domination plans with Retail World. It could be Retail Nook, or Retail Region, but not Retail World. Deal. Eddie bought a majority stake in Meadowhall and the pair joined forces to create Europe's biggest mall, in Sheffield.

Eddie then exported the Meadowhall blueprint to Germany in 1996, and opened the CentrO shopping complex in the rundown city of Oberhausen. In 1999 Meadowhall was sold to British Land for £1.17 billion, and Eddie received about £420 million.

Malcolm, meanwhile, returned to Britain and set up United Kitchens, which flopped (this happens!). It went into receivership in 2000 and Malcolm lost about £30 million. More successful was his Hull-based company, Stadium Developments, which built retail warehouses for companies like MFI.

Life without Qualifications

OK, so the brothers had a few bumps along the way, but these days they're not doing so badly. Malcolm paid £48 million for his 10,500-acre Warter Priory estate in 1998, beating off bids from Sir Mick Jagger and Sir Elton John, and *The Times* rated this property as one of the UK's ten most valuable houses. Eddie has a similarly rich and enjoyable lifestyle, buying luxury property left, right and centre. He also famously hired Girls Aloud to perform for his grandchildren at his 70th birthday party in 2008.

The brothers continue to build businesses and invest, whilst enjoying their luxury homes and exotic holidays, yet neither of them have ever felt the need to return to education and earn 'proper' qualifications. Funny thing, that.

Richard 'Dirty Des' Desmond, born 1951
Multimillionaire publisher of porn,
celebrity magazines and newspapers
Education: Left school at 14 without any formal qualifications

Nobody ever went bust appealing to the more 'low brow' tastes of the general public. I don't think so, anyway. And if, like Richard Desmond, you want to get rich selling pictures of bare, naked ladies in magazines called *Big Ones* and *Asian Babes*, you are allowed. Some people see Desmond as a fairly disreputable fellow, but I'm putting him in here because porn isn't *all* he's about. He had a classic entrepreneurial beginning, and he's now very rich and possibly the most powerful man in British publishing after Rupert Murdoch.

Richard Desmond was born into a middle-class, North London family in 1951. His father was sales director for Pearl & Dean, the cinema advertising company, but he went deaf and the young Richard had to spend many evenings helping him close sales deals – a strange but powerful initiation.

When Desmond was 12, his parents split up and he went to live with his mother in a flat above a shop in North London. He later said this glimpse of poverty fuelled his entrepreneurial ambitions.

Desmond went to Christ's College Grammar School, but was unhappy there, describing himself as 'fat and lonely'. He was rubbish at school, so left at 14.

Messing Around

As a fat 14-year old, Desmond got his first job stacking shelves at Woolworths. Then he worked as a cloakroom attendant with Thomson Newspapers – a fortuitous bit of messing around, because apparently he got friendly with the classified sales boss, who gave him a job selling ads over the phone. He was good at selling ads. He moved up and out. By 18 he was working as sales director (by some accounts) for a magazine about The Beatles.

The Business

By 21, Desmond owned property and two record shops. In 1974 – at the age of 23 – he had enough leverage to buy his first magazine. And no, it wasn't porn. It was a music title, called *International Musician*. His company, Northern & Shell, then expanded aggressively and launched other specialist magazines.

By 1982, Northern & Shell was big enough to build its own steel and glass office tower in London's Docklands. For the opening, Prince Philip did the honours. Just in time, you might say, because then Desmond got into porn.

The Big Business

In 1983 (he was, what, 32?) he secured the rights to publish *Penthouse* in the UK. It was the first in a stable of 'adult' titles, including *Asian Babes* and *Reader's Wives*. In 1993, Northern & Shell launched *OK!* magazine to go head-to-head with *Hello!*, and it's now Britain's biggest selling weekly, with 30 million readers worldwide.

In November 2000, Desmond continued to expand his media empire by buying Express Newspapers from United News & Media for £125 million, enlarging the group to include the *Daily Star* and *Daily Star Sunday*.

In 2004 he sold off the porn mags (although arguably the *Daily Star* still offers 'readers' their share of bare, naked ladies), but continues to rake in a few bob from Television X (a popular adult channel broadcast by Northern & Shell subsidiary, Portland TV), which turns over more than £30 million.

Life without Qualifications

In 2009, Desmond was the 44th equal richest man in Britain on the *Sunday Times Rich List,* with a net worth of £950 million. By all accounts, he is living a multimillionaire dream lifestyle and has property all over the place. At exactly 11am and 5pm each day, a liveried butler serves him a banana.

Graham Kirkham (Lord Kirkham to you) born 1944

Billionaire founder of DFS
Education: No formal qualifications – he failed his O levels,
all of them

Founder of the multimillion DFS furniture empire, Kirkham now enjoys a modest lifestyle as far as millionaires go. He only has two houses, for instance. And he furnishes them all with DFS furniture. Isn't that nice? A very happy, humble Yorkshire man, Kirkham achieved all his success without a single academic qualification.

Kirkham's story starts all in black and white. Adopted by a South Yorkshire miner and his wife when he was three weeks old, Graham Kirkham left school at 16. Like me, he won a place at grammar school (in his case, Maltby Grammar School), and like me he was rubbish. He was actually better at being rubbish than me – he needed five O levels to join the RAF but failed them all.

Messing Around

Kirkham's Messing Around phase was rather on the dull side and it didn't last all that long. After school, he got a job in a local furniture store and was married by the time he was 20. By the age of 22, he had two kids – at which point he rented a room above a snooker hall near Doncaster and started selling furniture. This was in 1969.

The Business

Having spent years messing around at a furniture store, Kirkham decided making furniture was incredibly easy and decided he'd make it himself to sell. He also realised that if he sold direct to the public, rather than from a shop, he could offer much lower prices. Such was the humble beginnings of DFS, which in those days was called the slightly less snappy, Northern Upholstery. Kirkham's company grew steadily for the next 14 years.

The Big Business

In 1983, aged 39, Kirkham saw his chance to expand when Direct Furnishing Supplies, one of his own suppliers, went bust with debts of £900,000, but with a turnover of £3 million. He bought it and assured customers that they wouldn't lose their deposits. Good to his word, he attracted a raft of new, loyal customers. He also got hip and opted to sling the plodding name, Northern Upholstery, in favour of the more zippy DFS.

Profits climbed dramatically. And when in 1993, DFS was floated on the stock market, it was valued at £271 million.

Bumps on the Road

In 1998, Kirkham needed his good old Yorkshire business sense after DFS announced its first drop in profits in 28 years. He saw what was wrong: DFS ad campaigns were targeting middle-aged couples, but it was the yuppie whippersnappers who were buying sofas. Also, his potential customers were kinky. He saw in a company survey that a third of DFS customers admitted to a leather fetish, so he spiced up the company's advertising. Near-naked models were draped over sofas, with flowers positioned strategically to cover naughty bits like in *Calendar Girls*. Sales bounced back and by 2000 DFS announced a 79 per cent profit increase.

But the revival was short-lived and Kirkham decided to take the chain private again, leveraging his family's own 9.46 per cent stake with £150 million of family funds in a £496 million deal.

He declared: 'I'm very conscious of our origins and the fact that we've done well with South Yorkshire values — being down to earth, having a very strong work ethic and loyalty, and knowing the value of money.' (And pandering to kinkiness, he might have added.) 'I've never got used to city people saying, "But Graham, it's only another £1 million…".'

Life without Qualifications

Kirkham has been modest with his millions. He owns just two homes: Grade II-listed Cantley Hall and a large house behind a six-foot-high wall in Sprotborough. He furnishes them with DFS sofas and nice pictures, including Gainsborough's 'Peasants Going to Market' (£3.5 million) and Constable's 'View of the Stour' (bought for £6.7 million).

In 1999 he was made a life peer as Baron Kirkham of Old Cantley in the County of South Yorkshire. He was one of the working peers recommended by then Tory leader, William Hague, who borrowed Kirkham's helicopter for electioneering from time to time.

Kirkham attributes a lot of his success to his family background. 'My whole life has been the luck of going to a good family,' he has said. But it's also worth noting that he got stuck into the real world from a young age, thanks to early educational failure. Could you imagine telling Kirkham that, despite all his success, he would have done better if he'd got a degree? No, didn't think so.

John Caudwell, born 1953
Billionaire mobile-phone tycoon
Education: Left college at 16 without taking his A levels

Self-made billionaire, John Caudwell, wasn't born into money and had many a crummy job sweeping up and selling used cars before he went into business and clocked up £1.46 billion. He enjoys a billionaire lifestyle many people dream about and guess what? He didn't go to university and quit his A levels after just three months. Bullied at school, Caudwell terminated his A levels at the age of 16, three months into studying Maths, Physics and Chemistry. He told interviewers he just wasn't academic. He wanted to be in the real world. Amen!

Messing Around

Caudwell studied at the 'university of life' by sweeping the floor of a pottery factory, working in a steel mill and being a nightclub bouncer. In 1970, he went into the Michelin Tyre Company as an apprentice engineer, which could have spelled a dull and boring end to a great business mind, but fortunately he set up a couple of businesses on the side (phew!).

The Business

What were these dazzling first businesses created by one of the UK's greatest business minds? A mail-order business selling motorcycle clothes from Caudwell's home and a grocery shop, which he ran with his wife. Not so exciting, then. And these first businesses didn't do so well, either. Did it matter? Not in the slightest – on the contrary, these first businesses taught Caudwell the vital lessons and mistakes that would eventually make him a billionaire.

Realising that self-employment was the place to be, Caudwell quit his Michelin job in 1980, paid off the debts these companies had acquired and went full-time into the used-car business. This was 'the business' mark two: Caudwell was growing and learning, as all entrepreneurs do, and his second venture was more successful. Seven years later, his Midland Garages had a staff of seven and a moderate turnover.

Bumps on the Road

One day in 1987, aged 34, Caudwell went into an electronics shop to buy a mobile phone for his business. In those days, mobile phones were still as big as bricks and considered a bit James Bond. The retailer was selling them for £1,600 each. But if you bought two you paid £1,350 each. That got Caudwell thinking. The mark-up on mobile phones must be huge. He got on the telephone and by the end of that afternoon he became an accredited Motorola dealer.

He bought 26 phones. It took eight months to sell them. He hired a manager to run the mobile business out of a back room in the car dealership, and a year later it was still running at a loss of around £1,000 a month. He kept going. In interviews, he attributed his tenacity to his background. 'I was brought up in a poor neighbourhood,' he said. 'I was bullied a lot… I think that made me into a bit of a fighter.' Monologue-ing, but we'll let him. He's earned it. Would he have been so tenacious if he hadn't got out of the 'hand-holding' education system early on and had a good taste of the real world? I don't know, but I'm pretty sure his Messing Around jobs gave him plenty of skills that pushed him forward.

In 1989, after two loss-making years, Caudwell's luck changed. Well, you could call it luck, but really he'd put himself in the path of opportunity. Mobile phones were going mainstream and Caudwell was in the right business to reap the benefits.

The Big Business

By 1991, the Caudwell Group turnover hit £13 million, making it the UK's largest independent distributor of mobile phones. Caudwell was turning over £1 billion by 2000. By 2003, he employed over 8,000 staff worldwide and sold 26 phones per minute.

Caudwell was bent on creating the largest private telecoms group in the world when the market slowed and stymied his plans. Feeling he was on somewhat of a sinking ship, he decided to duck out of the mobile phone business and look for opportunities elsewhere. In 2006, he sold the Caudwell Group for £1.46 billion to private equity firms and tried to find solace where he could. In his 50-room Jacobean mansion, for instance, and enjoying his helicopter, plane, yachts, Bentleys and motorbikes.

Life without Qualifications

Now Caudwell spends most of his time supporting his charity, Caudwell Children, donating to the NSPCC and doing 1,000-mile charity bike rides. Not such a disreputable lifestyle for a man who purposely quit formal education at the first opportunity.

PART 3

Education for Entrepreneurs

CHAPTER SEVEN

Entry Requirements:
Are You an Entrepreneur?

Are you all fired up now? I hope so, because it's time for the nitty-gritty – how to do it.

There is no secret formula here. A lot of this is just common sense, and maybe a lot of it you have heard it all before, but I'm going to relate key points to my own experience so you can see how entrepreneurialism works in the real world.

Also, I want you to be encouraged by this part of the book. It should fill you with confidence. 'Because,' I was going to say, 'it's actually very simple and easy.' But that's not what I mean, exactly. It's hard to describe. Setting up and running a successful business is not simple, and it's often difficult and hard work. But it doesn't *feel* difficult and hard, not the way other things in life feel difficult and hard.

I started to call it 'easy-hard' work, for want of a better term, until I read about an American psychologist (Mihaly Csikszentmihalyi) who in the 1960s began studying the states of mind of painters, athletes, craftsmen, mountain climbers and the like. They get so absorbed in what they're doing that they go into a kind of trance and lose all consciousness of themselves and the world around them. One word he came up with for this state was 'autotelic', from the Greek words *auto*, for 'self', and *telos*, for 'goal or purpose'. Self-directed, in other words. Then he just called it 'flow', and that made him famous.

Flow. That's what I mean. When you're setting up and running your own business it may be lots of hard work, but you don't notice it at the time because you're in flow. Maybe not 24 hours a day, every day, but often, and usually when you most need it.

With that in mind, it's pointless to try and define an airtight manual for setting up a business, because every person is different and every business opportunity is different. Also, when you're in flow, chances are you're going to be doing the right thing anyway because that's part of what being in flow is all about. However, you have to start somewhere and practical advice works, so I'm going to offer as much practical advice drawn from my own experience as I can, starting with the question that's on everybody's mind when they think about starting a business, namely: 'Have I got what it takes?'

The ability to set up a business and get rich is not some rare gift, like extra-sensory perception, or bone-setting. If you've read this far you'll have begun to appreciate that there is nothing very special about me. And yet the 'noise' out there on the subject gives people exactly the opposite impression. There is a great deal of mumbo jumbo around on the psychological make-up of entrepreneurs. Behavioural scientists study entrepreneurs as if they were bizarre and puzzling aberrations of nature.

What is an Entrepreneur?

I had to chuckle at a study a few years ago by this mega-team of researchers. They had guys from the Twin Research Unit at St. Thomas' Hospital in London. They had guys from the Tanaka School of Business at Imperial College in London. And they had guys from Case Western Reserve University in Cleveland. With a team like that you'd think they were launching an expedition to Jupiter. But no, they were searching for the 'entrepreneurial gene'.

They looked for self-employment in 609 pairs of identical twins (who share all their genes) and 657 pairs of same-sex non-identical twins (who share about half of their genes). They looked at whether one twin being an entrepreneur increased the chance of their co-twin becoming an entrepreneur. What they found blew them away: there was more copycatting among identical twins than non-identical twins! The conclusion was astounding: entrepreneurialism is genetic! They decided that something like 50 per cent of someone's propensity to become self-employed could be attributed to their genes.

The press I read around that study suggested all sorts of wild ramifications. If they could just map this fabled 'entrepreneurial gene', recruiters in the business world would have a fool-proof forecasting tool in their search for 'the next big talent'. Venture capitalists would have a field day. Instead of having to rely on meticulous research, years of experience and gut instinct in choosing where to invest their money, all they'd need to do is collect hair samples!

This is of course all very silly. I'm no expert on the psychology of identical twins, but it stands to reason that if two people look identical from birth and get treated as basically interchangeable because of that, you're going to get a fair bit of extra copycatting in that group. Genetic proof, indeed!

Here is another conclusion you could draw, based on this silliness. I never met a Thai, Pakistani or Bangladeshi person who came to the UK, marched off the plane and headed straight down to the local benefits office to pore over the forms to see what they could get. The ones I know opened a business. Or took over a business that their mum, dad, auntie, uncle or cousin started. Or they got two or three menial jobs so they could scrape some cash together, get the lie of the land, and then opened their own business.

Is it because Thai, Pakistani and Bangladeshi people who move to the UK are genetically programmed to be entrepreneurs? No. It's because often where they come from life is brutally hard and dangerous and unpredictable. In other countries, if you find yourself without money and your family network can't support you, you don't just sign on and get a council flat. What happens is that getting something to eat for you and your children suddenly becomes really, really tricky. Avoiding horrible, disgusting and fatal diseases like cholera becomes a daily, all-consuming challenge, on top of all the other daily, all-consuming challenges. Life gets very ugly very quickly and then most likely stops.

Deeply embedded in the perceptions of many foreign people who move to the UK is this fundamental truth: nobody is going to provide me with a living. They know, as deeply and as surely as they know they need air to breathe, that they have no one to rely on but themselves. And they're amazed that they can get on with improving their lot so easily in this country.

There is a whole industry devoted to the psychology of entrepreneurs, and I believe it's all mumbo jumbo. Respected university professors blow big tax-payer-provided grants on surveys and studies into the mental make-up of people who started their own businesses and got rich. They come up with definitive lists of character traits and detailed profiles based on upbringing and other environmental factors. Entrepreneurs, they say, are more comfortable than normal human beings with risk. Entrepreneurs, they say, have a specific way of thinking – 'wiggly' is one word I've come across – which throws up a greater number of solutions and options. Entrepreneurs, they say, experienced a profound 'shaping' event in their childhoods, like a bereavement, a move to another city where all the kids laughed at them, or perhaps a slightly less than satisfactory change in the décor of their bedrooms. Entrepreneurs, they say, are usually the youngest of siblings, and therefore more ready to rebel and break the mould. Entrepreneurs, they say, have a greater need to control their environment than ordinary dolts.

Rubbish.

You can buy huge academic tomes written by learned big wigs in the field of organisational psychology. One of these guys, Alexander Zelaznick, is a distinguished professor emeritus of psychology at Harvard Business School. He said that years of interviewing entrepreneurs led him to the dramatic conclusion that they simply did not feel risk, or weigh consequences, in the same way as other people. He told *The New York Times* in 1986: 'To understand the entrepreneur you first have to understand the psychology of the juvenile delinquent.'

(This is good news! Who, at some point in their lives, has not been a juvenile delinquent?)

On it goes. And for every glittering, hard-won characteristic on their lists, up crops a Bill Gates, a Richard Branson or a John Mudd who plays awkward and doesn't fit.

Mumbo jumbo. Don't listen to it! On one hand, I suppose, it's just another example of the useless, parasitic, navel-gazing that goes on in the ivory towers of academia. But on the other hand I find it seriously annoying and harmful because it promotes this myth that entrepreneurs are by nature somehow strange and set apart – delinquent, even! Deformed! They're not. Have you got what it takes? Are you a mum? Most mums I know have more fortitude, skill and resourcefulness than most entrepreneurs I know. If we could just get a few more mums to start businesses I believe Britain would become a tiger economy to rival China.

The myth of the entrepreneur as a rare and strange creature gets repeated and amplified in our culture because so many people, consciously or not, feel just that teensy bit stupid that they stuck with their jobs and didn't set up in business for themselves. They prefer stories of failure to stories of success because these stories justify their own timidity. They feed on gossip about how vicious, crooked and vain rich people are because it allows them to feel superior.

For exactly this reason, sometimes even closest friends and family aren't 100 per cent supportive of your entrepreneurial ventures. They perhaps don't actively want you to fail, but they may be secretly pleased if you do. Some philosophy about playing it safe will be satisfactorily realised. The way the universe is ordered in their minds will be reinforced. The applecart will have been put right-side-up again.

Have you got what it takes? I bet you do. However, there are two personal qualities that you definitely need to set up a business and get rich and we need to talk about them for a bit. I don't mean some abnormal lust for risk or wiggly thinking or overreaching control freakery. These are simple things you need, and if you don't have them you can get them. They are 1) self-belief and 2) the ability to sell. A bit boring, a bit predictable, I know, but it's true.

Have you got what it takes?

Self-belief

You have to believe in yourself *and* in the product or service you are selling if you are going to set up a business and get rich. There is no way around this. You have to believe that:

Your goal is worthwhile

You can achieve it

You deserve to get rich

You Can Achieve It

You have to believe in your enterprise, but it's just as important to believe in yourself. You must know, feel, trust that you can achieve it. I'm one of those people who have plenty of confidence now – I was anything but when I left school. Any shred of confidence I did have had been whittled away in the 6 years of KEGS. The confidence I now enjoy I had to learn, and you can too. You're going to need that, and lots of it. If you're not that confident, you can *get* more confident. It is a thing you can work on and get better at. And I'm not talking about being ridiculously, annoyingly confident or delusional. I'm talking about gaining freedom from destructive, paralysing, self-defeating thought processes.

One way of breaking out of those psychological chains is neuro-linguistic programming (NLP). This is a fascinating field that looks at how our brains become habituated to certain thoughts and responses in an actually physical way – physical as in neurons sending electro-chemical messages via certain pathways in your brain. We're talking about real things here, electricity, tissue and substances.

Your brain is a wondrous computer and organ, but it can be guided and improved. You can shut down bad habits of thinking and launch and strengthen good habits of thinking. What are bad habits of thinking? We all fall prey to them. These are the thoughts that travel those well-worn neural pathways to dead ends. Always dead ends.

I think of these as rubbish rollercoasters. The riders of these rubbish rollercoasters are the usual suspects: blame, self-justification, complaining, defensiveness, resentment, envy, etc. These bad and useless mental habits shuffle into the rollercoaster car, bitching and moaning, and off they go. They whiz through the neural pathway for a while, round a few sharp corners and a loop or two, and it feels kind of satisfying. It scratches some kind of itch. But then, because it's a rubbish rollercoaster, the ride comes to an abrupt end, where it always does, in a shallow, stinking puddle of bile.

What a rubbish rollercoaster!

Good thinking habits have a dramatically different result. This rollercoaster is way over on the other side of the funfair. Its passengers are a more upmarket lot. They look great. They are well-dressed and attractive. These riders are mental habits like hope, responsibility, courage, affection, trust, curiosity, imagination, truth-telling and other positive thought-processes. This rollercoaster whizzes around and gives you a real sense of elation. Plus it goes on for a lot longer. Sometimes it connects up with other rollercoasters and doesn't seem to want to stop. When it does you find you're in a much better place than you were before, characterised by knowledge, empathy, connection, understanding, empowerment, passion, energy and clarity, to name a few.

I have a solidly scientific, practical and empirical cast of mind. I like reasons and evidence. I think the universe is ultimately intelligible. I don't go in for crystals, astrology, ley lines, reincarnation or patchouli oil (then again, I haven't really investigated the market for this stuff!). And yet I have no trouble at all banging on about self-belief and its importance, no matter how New-Agey it might *sound*.

Your thoughts create tomorrow. They do. What you focus on grows. You end up where you want to end up. What you conceive you will achieve (I didn't mean for that to rhyme, it just did). The problem is, most people muddle along with no detailed destination in mind. They look ahead and all they see is fog. There may be a few dim shapes – some nice holidays, a better-paid or more interesting job, a satisfying relationship, a comfortable retirement – but nothing very specific, and certainly nothing bold. People go rudderless like this for one or a combination of four reasons:

- They don't realise that they're *allowed* to create the sort of tomorrow they want.
- They feel that it is somehow presumptuous to try and create the sort of tomorrow they want.
- They actually have no idea what sort of tomorrow they want.
- They don't believe that defining and articulating the tomorrow they want will make any difference.

There is hope for all of these people, except for those in the fourth category. These people believe that life happens *to* them and there is nothing to be done about it. They are trapped in a perfect self-fulfilling reality. Because they believe this, that is what comes true. This is a great shame. These people are missing out on the chance to perform real magic, conjuring up a stupendous result from nothing.

Entrepreneurs understand this. They know that their thoughts create tomorrow. They also know that tomorrow will be created whether it's their thoughts doing the creating or someone else's. Entrepreneurs take the bull by the horns. They insist on being the ones doing the creating.

Now, it's beyond the scope of this book to go into neuro-linguistic programming and the specific techniques for bolstering your confidence and articulating your vision. The point I'm trying to make is that if you don't have the necessary mental furniture you can get it. There are lots of good books and articles and seminars and CDs out there. Some of them will have names that make you cringe, and you may be reluctant to open them up on crowded trains, but never mind. If it works, it's good.

Here's one little story about this. I said earlier that I'm one of those lucky people who have plenty of confidence, which is true. Then again, I've always been an avid reader of self-improvement books. There is a simple reason for this: they make me feel positive and they give me useful advice. Some of them turn out to be a bit snake-oily, but so what? Even those ones usually contain some nugget you can store away for use later.

I'm a particularly big fan of Tony Robbins. Yes, he's American and yes, he's a bit schmaltzy. A typical line from one of his books would go something like:

'I realised I'd finally made it when I was flying my jet helicopter over Los Angeles and noticed what looked like a huge traffic jam, the biggest I'd ever seen. Then I realised these cars were lining up to get into the auditorium where I was speaking!'

Pure schmaltz, but so what? Either it works or it doesn't, and for me it works.

Anyway, once, back when I was still living at home, I was lounging around reading a self-help book (it may even have been a Tony Robbins book, like *Awaken the Giant Within: How to take immediate control of your mental, emotional, physical and financial destiny*) and my Uncle Bob, a guy who was only sort of an uncle but who was an occasional and welcome visitor, saw me reading this and made fun of me. 'What are you reading that rubbish for?' he scoffed. 'Load of old cobblers!'

I liked and respected Uncle Bob. He seemed like a confident and successful guy. While I banged around in a beat-up Nissan Cherry, he had a brand new Ford Sierra. I can't remember what I said in response, but it didn't put me off reading self-improvement books. About a year and a half later he called round again. His Ford Sierra was in the drive when I got home from work, and I pulled up beside him – in my new Ferrari.

Yes, it's possible to read too much into these things. But I believe Uncle Bob's response is worth noting. If you want to improve yourself and take control of your destiny you are going to get sneers and hostility. Now it's just possible that Uncle Bob scoffed out of concern. He may have perceived my book as some sort of quasi-religious fakery and didn't want me to be taken in by it. Or that may have been a *part* of what he felt. It's just as likely, however, that he was partaking in a peculiarly British reflex, which is to ladle scorn over any obvious effort at self-improvement.

We tend to see it as foolish, unseemly, in bad taste – in the same class as over-exuberance in a church service. We're taught in a thousand ways not to stick our necks out. Every dinner table, classroom, office and factory in the land has their eagle-eyed, sharp-tongued monitors just waiting to see who needs to be brought down a peg or two. It's not just: 'So you think you're better than everybody else, do you?' It's far more heinous: 'You *want* to *be* better than everybody else!'

Deadbeats and downers need deadbeats and downers around them. Anybody who isn't a deadbeat or a downer is a real threat to their authority. They need to be mocked and shown up and brought down a peg or two. Uncle Bob's scoffing, and the invitation or warning it contained for me to drop this self-improvement lark and rejoin the club of cool people who accept their lot, is not a million miles away from the kids who pressure frightened little wimps into joining them smoking out by the bike shed.

Self-belief is an entrepreneur's most precious commodity. It's way more important than capital. Get it and keep it. Nurture and protect it, fiercely.

You've Got to Sell

Have you got what it takes? This is the last thing on this subject. It's a kind of a nuts and bolts thing, but it's absolutely essential.

You have to be able to sell. I was exceedingly lucky. I had two deep, formative experiences in my Messing Around phase – cheese and eggs and timeshares – that gave me an early and solid grounding in the essential art of selling.

Oh no, you say! I'm a shrinking wallflower! I'm an ideas person! This is exactly what you'd hoped to avoid: all that grubby, grasping, unseemly business of selling. It's practically a dirty word these days. Say *salesman* and it conjures up terrible images of devious, pushy, thrusting, greasy, brash, spotty estate agents. Nobody in their right minds – nobody *proper* – would want to go into sales these days, would they? *That's why,* you sob, *I went to university!*

Sorry, you've got to sell.

Selling is important even if your business is not *about* selling. Even if you're not going door-to-door selling cleaning supplies (franchises for that type of business are going for between £7,000 and £23,000, by the way, so there's clearly money in it). Perhaps you believe your business offers connection and dignity and isn't about the cold, unfeeling business of generating hard cash.

It's true that many businesses are founded on ethical and worthy principles. But those principles don't come before selling. Great principles are what you *end up* following once you have *sold* your service to the elderly person or, more likely, to their suspicious, stressed-out and cash-strapped kids. Customers have no idea you're offering connection and dignity. You have to convince them and then close the deal. No matter what service or thing you offer, I am here to inform you that *selling* is *exactly* what your business is about. Without *selling* you don't *have* a business.

And it is a skill that you will use at all levels. Not just in getting customers, but in hiring good staff. Yes, you'll need to sell the business to them, too. Especially in hiring and training the staff (whose job it will be to get customers) *to sell* for you. These are the most important people in your business. Also in negotiating contracts with suppliers. Yes, you need to sell the business to them, too, if you want to negotiate better rates. Same with negotiating finance, should you need it, from banks.

To realise your business's potential and to reach as many customers as possible, you're going to have to do some serious selling. And then, when it's time to look beyond your county and reach out to the millions of customers all over the UK and Europe, you're going to need to franchise your business and offer those opportunities to other lucky entrepreneurs – *for sale*.

Here's an example of why the skill of selling is important. This is just one example of many. Let's say you've got your concept – home-care. You've worked out roughly how you can provide the service. Now you need some customers. You've put some marketing material together – it looks so great! – and you've leafleted one whole neighbourhood in your town where some informal research has led you to believe that there are bound to be some takers. And out you go to conquer the world! By 11 o'clock you've done 30 homes, and you've had 13 no-answers, two time-wasters, four polite and apologetic 'no thank yous' and 11 slammed doors.

You are crushed, utterly and irrevocably.

You sit down on a bench and the awful truth dawns – this is never, ever going to work. There is not a single person in this town who wants your service. It was all a stupid idea.

Now, with some basic grounding in sales you would look at it quite differently. You may even be quite upbeat: after all, you've had four nice chats and it's only 11 am. You'd know that you still have nearly 70 per cent of your target audience to reach that day, so there are lots and lots of reasons to be hopeful. Also, even if nobody says yes today, you're only just taking the first baby steps and anyway the first customer is always the hardest and it gets much easier when you've got a few.

Resilience. You need this. It's not the same as self-belief. It's less profound than self-belief, but it's just as important. It is the technical understanding, based on training and experience, that you're going to get a lot more people saying 'no' than yes', and that it *isn't you* they are rejecting.

Now it's not that you have to be the best seller in your company, or that you will always have to be doing all the selling. It's more that you're going to have to get the ball rolling by selling, and you're going to have to keep it rolling by selling. And most importantly you're going to have to never, ever forget how central the process and skill of selling is to any business, especially your business. And furthermore, you're going to have to be able to tell at any moment whether your business is doing it well or not, and if not, to urgently do something about it.

Recently I invested in *Raw Business* magazine. I was impressed with the guy behind it, Bradley Chapman, a real visionary entrepreneur and master salesman. This is a new magazine in a crowded marketplace, at a time when the print publishing business seems to be dying on its feet. Leaf through the magazine and, as well as in-depth profiles about fascinating people, what will strike you is how *stuffed* with ads it is. He's got a team of highly motivated salespeople working the phones old-style. It is beautiful to see. *Raw Business* is not *The Economist*, or *Harvard Business Review*. It's relatively unknown and a bit rough around the edges. But it's raw and full of energy – and it generates *£45,000 of ad revenue every issue*!

You've got to sell!

But it's OK. I have good news. Just like how it is with self-belief, if you're rubbish at it, you can get better. You can acquire those skills. They are not entirely God-given. They can be learned and honed. Read books, listen to CDs, take a course, attend a seminar. You're starting out on an entirely new life – you can afford a morning or afternoon or a weekend in a strange context with odd people learning something new and useful. Practise and have fun with it. Maybe you will never be a high-flyer. Maybe never a 'natural'. But by learning some techniques and by practising and improving over time you can be 100 per cent, 200 per cent or even 300 per cent better than you are now.

And your business will reward you for it. Lady Lucre loves a salesperson.

CHAPTER EIGHT

Freshman Year:
How To Start Your Business

Choosing Your Business Venture

The specific venture you choose will arise out your own situation: where you are, what you can see, what you know, who you know, what you can do, what you like doing and, most importantly, who you are.

You may be young or you may be not so young. Either way, this chapter will help.

If you're young and have little or no experience in the world of work, you need to complete your Messing Around phase. Get a job. Do it well. Think of yourself as a spy. Get to know people. Find out how the business works, how the industry works. Also, try new things and find out what you're good at. Don't hang with the losers and downers. Don't nurse some tragic sense of grievance and pointlessness. This isn't your life, this is Messing Around. There are specific things you're going to take away from it. It won't last long. Soonish, put yourself forward for promotion. When you've got what you need from that job, get another one. Repeat steps above as necessary. Meanwhile, read this chapter and keep your eyes open.

If you're not so young and have been working for a while, or maybe too long, you probably already have some ideas. Your feet are itchy and your finger keeps going to the trigger. That's great but, still, read this. My experience has taught me five basic principles that you can apply to your choice of venture. I believe

that following these principles will set you immediately apart
from the herd of wannabe entrepreneurs out there whose failures
we hear so much about.

In summary, these principles are:

- Be narrow
- Come in low
- Be unoriginal
- Be early
Believe in your business

1. Be Narrow

*'Enter through the narrow gate. For wide is the gate
and broad is the road that leads to destruction.'*
(Matthew 7:13)

That's Jesus. He was talking about the salvation of your soul,
which is not what I'm talking about. In fact, I should mention
before you carry on reading: Jesus also said that it's easier for a
camel to get through the eye of a needle than for a rich man to
enter the Kingdom of God. He may have been speaking
figuratively. I, for one, certainly hope so. But the Kingdom of
Heaven isn't my department. You're going to have to take it up
with Him when the time comes.

My department is starting up successful businesses (and
getting rich) and I mention Jesus' advice above because it's
excellent for starting a successful business too. Enter through the
narrow gate. Avoid the big, wide gate everybody's heading for.
Look for the chink nobody's noticed.

Think *niche*.

What do I mean?

When people think of starting a business, most dream the
impossible dream. They wrack their brains for that new device
or product every consumer in the world will immediately want

to buy. I call this the *Sliced Bread Syndrome*, as in: 'That's the best thing since sliced bread!' People fall into the Sliced Bread Syndrome because they have a very naive notion – a myth, actually – of how to get rich.

It's a myth that starts from childhood, where we start picking up the stories of all the legendary mega-rich, like Henry Ford, who created a car everyone could buy, or Bill Gates, who created an operating system for every computer. This myth gets strengthened by TV shows like *Dragons' Den*, where the wannabe entrepreneurs are all touting products which, however silly, are geared for the mass consumer market, whether it's non-spill, travel-friendly dog-food bowls or remote-controlled, wheelie-bin lid-lifters. Most of the start-ups and 'hot' new companies that get any press or air time at all tend to fall into this category.

The fact is, of all the people who start successful businesses and get rich, a tiny proportion of them do it with Sliced Bread, or the Next Big Thing. The Henry Ford and Bill Gates stories, while true, are so majorly not the norm that they are about as instructive as fairy tales. *Dragons' Den* creates a huge impression that Sliced Bread is where the action is, but that's only because it wouldn't work on TV otherwise.

For it to be good TV, *you*, the viewer, have to engage with the wannabe entrepreneur and you can only do that if *you* think, sitting there as one of a few million mass consumers, that maybe he or she is onto something. If the *Dragons' Den* entrepreneurs were all going after the real money, say with software for 2D barcode printers or radio-frequency transponders for tracking rubbish lorries, ratings would plummet and the Beeb would have to pull the show.

There are three main reasons why going for Sliced Bread is a non-starter in terms of starting a successful business and getting rich. The first is that Sliced Bread is subjective. You may think it's Sliced Bread and your mates might think it's Sliced Bread, but for the masses it might be just another skeleton-hand back-scratcher.

The second reason is that it costs a lot of money to communicate your message to the masses. Let's say you make a mean pasta sauce. All your mates say it's the best. You should go commercial, they say. You think, wow, the market is huge. Every pasta-eating grocery shopper in the land. What's that? You do some wishful Googling and conclude that there are 19 million pasta-eating, grocery-list decision makers in the UK right now. You haven't even considered all the pasta-eating, grocery-list decision makers in America, Canada, Australia and New Zealand! In the UK alone you've got 19 million people eager to hear that you've got a product that will wipe the floor with Paul Newman, Lloyd Grossman, Linda McCartney, Uncle Tom Cobley and all the rest of them. But how are you going to communicate with all these potential customers? The requisite marketing campaign would blow millions before you'd even sterilised a jar.

The third reason is competition. 19 million is certainly a tasty prize, and because it's a tasty prize you may be sure you're not the only one eyeing it. The fact that you're a 'little guy' offering something unique won't help. Here are some of the other little guys you might find yourself 'jostling' with for the attentions of your 19 million (soundtrack of doom, please): Kraft, Mars, Unilever, General Mills and Premier Foods (they do Branston Pickle, Hovis bread and Sharwood's Indian sauces, by the way).

No, no. Retire from that fight. Wide is the gate and broad is the road (and strewn with linguini) that leads to bankruptcy. The problem here is that you identify with your pasta sauce. Your excellent pasta sauce is actually a little piece of you that you want to send out onto the world stage in hopes of standing ovations. But the pasta sauce business is only a little about pasta sauce, and it's nothing about you. More than anything it's about marketing, distribution, process manufacturing and economies of scale, stuff you've probably never even thought about before and which will take a lifetime, or a very expensive team of experts, to learn.

The story of John Mudd is instructive here. John Mudd decided to launch a new brand of crisps, and he did – The Real Crisps Company. It was still going the last time I looked. This wasn't a Sliced Bread fairy tale. Mudd knew crisps. He'd spent years in the business, ending up as marketing chief for Bensons Crisps. He felt sure there would be a market for traditional, hand-cooked crisps. Other people were doing it. The Kettle brand was here from America. So, in his fifties, he scraped £135,000 together, including his £25,000 severance package from Bensons and £100,000 from the bank, leased a factory and launched.

That was 1997. He worked and worked on those crisps for two years. He got some customers in pubs and shops, but there was a quality issue. The second-hand cookers weren't up to the job and the nice home-cooked crisps were greasy. The customers were drifting off in search of other crisp solutions. He knew how to fix the problem, but crisp-factory equipment is expensive and he'd already burned most of his original £135,000. So when a bigger company offered to buy his company, there didn't seem to be any other choice. In 1999 he sold, retaining just 16 per cent of shares, and ended up taking a job as sales and marketing manager in the company he founded.

Is this a happy ending or a sad ending? It's hardly a terrible one, that's for sure. Mudd's name is hardly mud. To say otherwise would be to throw salt in his wounds. And vinegar. That 16 per cent stake could be worth something if the company is doing OK and if anybody wants to buy his shares. But on the other hand, for an entrepreneur to have to relinquish ownership of a wealth machine, even a bit of ownership, is a bitter outcome. I think this is what happens when you try and launch fast-moving consumer goods for the mass market.

Think *niche*. The crisp-eating public is not niche. Doing VAT returns is not niche, but doing it just for IT contractors is. It means you've got a defined community. You know where they hang out, what they talk about and what worries them. You know how to get in front of them with your message.

Here's a good example of niche. Books. All kinds of different books for the general public. The general public who *work in offices*. Ted Smart did that. For nearly 20 years Ted Smart and a friend ran a small publishing company. They published more than 600 titles, but apart from a smash hit with a big glossy book about Diana's wedding, it was a real slog shifting those books. One day out of desperation he sent a clerk down Guildford High Street with a bag of books to try and sell to people in offices. The clerk sold £400 worth. Smart left his publishing business and set up a new company just selling books, all kinds of books, to people in offices. They'd set up a table, display the books, come back a week later and take orders. Because he bought the books outright, as opposed to sale or return, he was able to negotiate discounts from the publishers. Smart's company, The Book People, was turning over £97 million in 2008.

2. Come in Low

To launch a new line of crisps, and to get them onto the shelves, and to keep them there long enough for people to try them burns an awful lot of money for an awful long time. So my advice is this: choose the sort of business that doesn't require masses of start-up capital. That allows you to get some customers right away, get some cash flowing and grow from there – organically, as you can afford to. The seed funding for my business, which turns over more than £70 million now, was ten quid. That's it. Every other investment I made to grow the business came out of the profits of my business.

Remember Roma and the Trannies of Levenshulme? Clients could chill out, read a book, try on outfits, whatever, for £80 a day? All she had to do was open her door. This is a pure example of *niche* and *coming in low*.

A service is generally a lot less costly to launch than a product, especially if it's something you already know how to do or can learn quickly. Gardening, cleaning and tax returns come to mind. Chatting with old people. Cutting hair. Walking dogs, growing vegetables, painting houses. Selling (we'll come back to selling).

Coming in low doesn't mean *come in with low standards,*

however. It is still the case, in these high-tech and complicated days, that providing a service well, for the price agreed, on time, with a smile, draws gasps of delight and relief.

Nor should *coming in low* mean *coming in cheap*. I started off cheap, too cheap, and as a result I ended up with too many bargain-basement-dwellers. These people make awful clients. The less they paid the more they demanded and the more fickle they turned out to be. As soon as the next cheap thing came along they were off. In hindsight I should have pitched the price midway between the cheapest and dearest of my nearest competitors. This probably would have worked because I made myself seem like a national company (it's way easier these days, thanks to websites, to create that impression). I also believe that coming in so cheaply actually put clients off. Hardly anyone buys on price alone, and being the absolute cheapest doesn't always send out the signal you want.

Niche and *coming in low* should not mean *small*, either. Once I settled on a formula – outsourced accounting for IT contractors – my market expanded instantly from Manchester to the whole country. You have to start small, but you can't stay there if you want to get rich. If you want to get rich you have to choose a customer base that is infinitely expandable. Now, there is a special set of challenges attached to this sort of business. It starts with you providing a service. But if you're any good and you've chosen the service well, you're quickly going to grow beyond your capacity to deliver. But that's OK. That's good. Later we'll talk about how to expand and duplicate yourself so that you can grow.

3. Be Unoriginal

Beware the Sliced Bread Syndrome. Don't go off in search of new ideas. For one thing, you're going to have to develop the idea, and that doesn't mean spending hours mooning about how great it is and how rich you'll be. It means working the idea out in concrete detail from concept to delivery. Once you've done that you're going to have to test it extensively. And that's not the half of it. If, at that point, you're lucky enough not to have discovered that somebody else has already done it, to get anybody to buy it you're going to have to re-educate them. You'll have to spend even more precious time and effort convincing people and getting them to think like you do.

Why bother? This is business, not a debating society. It's so much easier to copy good ideas already out there that are proven to work, and to do them better, more cheaply or with a twist. That way, somebody else has already done the hard bit. Yes, there's a lot of glory in coming up with the Next Big Thing. Same with inventing. But there isn't a lot of money in it. Do you want to be remembered, or do you want to be rich?

For instance, one of the easiest ways of setting up in business for yourself is to buy a franchise. That means you pay a sum and start trading as a local branch of an existing business. The milkshake-machine seller, Ray Kroc, absolutely perfected the franchise model after he bought his burger business from the MacDonald brothers in the '50s. You can get a franchise for just about any sort of business: pet supplies, financial consulting, coffee shops, education, any sort of retail – even pig farming in Thailand.

Franchising has certain advantages if you're in a hurry. The product is already there, the marketing machine is already up and running and the franchisor will train you in a proven business system – if the franchise is any good – and provide ongoing technical support. There are disadvantages too, though. You will need money up front, anywhere from a couple of thousand to over a hundred thousand, depending on the strength of the franchise brand and the volume of turnover the franchisor has come to expect.

Many franchisors peg the initial investment at between £20k and £40k, which is far from cheap if you're young and starting out, but may be manageable if you're older and have savings or a house to re-mortgage. That sum may or may not include vehicles or other necessary equipment. Also it's not *quite* your business. The product, the marketing and the basic processes are all dictated from above.

Still, don't sniff at it. Franchising works for a lot of people and, as in all entrepreneurial activity, success will be down to your own drive and competence in selling and organisation. It may be a good interim move, and a way to take your abilities out for a spin.

Another good way of being unoriginal is to identify a product made somewhere else, like in the US, and to secure the rights to distribute or manufacture the product here.

4. Be Early

I firmly believe that you can do just about anything, in just about any sector, and do it better than the incumbents. You can squeeze a fried chicken joint in between two existing fried chicken joints and still stand out. That's because, as I've said before, the basic standard of customer service and quality in this country is eye-wateringly bad.

However, I have one more piece of advice on the subject of choosing your venture, and it is this: if you have your eyes set on meteoric growth, choose a sector that's new and growing, the way computer chips and mobile phones were once new and growing and the way railroads and e-commerce were once new and growing. Watch out for those sectors where increasing media and consumer interest, combined with inward investment, political posturing and demographic pressure all combine to create one of those frenzies that make the surface of the sea of commerce boil.

Back in 1996 when I started, the dotcom bubble was still ballooning over our heads like a big, wobbly stadium roof. I didn't know anything about networks or software but I did know about tax returns. So I offered that to IT contractors and... bingo!

So what's hot now? Well, I'm not geared up to provide a

detailed sector by sector analysis, but I do have two suggestions:

1. Greening the UK building stock. That's right. We have one of the leakiest, most expensive, least energy efficient collection of homes, schools, offices, shops, malls and hospitals in the developed world, and the government is dead set on changing that. It wants all new homes to be 'zero-carbon' by 2016 and it wants the whole lot, new and existing, to be emitting no carbon for heat and power by 2050.

    This is a massive, and possibly unrealistic, undertaking. It's called the Great British Refurb. So what's it got to do with me, you ask? I'm not a builder, nor do I sell double glazing. Maybe not, but could you? What complementary skills would you need to buy, beg, borrow or steal to do it? Beyond that, what services – marketing, IT, legal, design, financial, catering, cleaning, recruitment, secretarial – might suddenly be in demand for the builders, architects, quantity surveyors, consultants, product manufacturers and technology suppliers who are already scrambling to understand this huge market that is, literally, on their doorsteps? Just an idea…

2. Old people. The number of people over pensionable age in the UK, according to Age Concern, is forecast to rise to around 14 million by 2031, from around 11.4 million in 2006. The media calls it an 'age-quake'. The proportion is shifting, so that the number of old people is growing and the number of young people is shrinking. Even now, for the first time ever, the number of people over 65 exceeds those under 16.

    Whatever else this demographic phenomenon might mean, it's an entrepreneur's dream. Old people need young people to look after them, so you have a steadily increasing demand, coupled with a steadily decreasing supply. Brilliant! They need to be housed, fed, entertained, chatted to, driven around and medically treated. They want to learn, read, travel, meet each other, go out on the town and so on. The possibilities here are endless. I just checked one web directory for franchises going for sale and spotted ten right away dealing with home care.

This next piece of advice I offer with extreme hesitation. The advice is this. You *could* pay attention to new technology in the wings, like fuel cells, hydrogen cars, printed photovoltaics and nanotechnology. And you *could* begin to wonder and ask and research how, if these things go mainstream like the internet and mobile phones did, the way we do things will change and then consider what new products or services might be in demand as a result. You *could* do that. But I hesitate with this advice because for a lot of people this future-gazing could become mesmerising, an end in itself, and also an infatuated search for Sliced Bread and ultimately just an excuse for not getting on with it.

So maybe never mind about that one.

Just dive in, and dive in early.

5. Believe in your Business

Let's say you've chosen a business venture that ticks all the boxes. It's narrow, cheap, unoriginal and early. You can start small and you can go big. Maybe you've even lined up your first customer or three. Excellent! Now pause and take stock. Do you believe in it yet? Really believe? Or are you wracked with doubts? It may be that, intellectually, you can see that what you're offering represents decent value but somehow your emotions haven't jumped on board. Emotionally, you're freaked out that someone's going to nail you for a fraud, that they're going to take what you're offering by one end, hold it up and say: 'Look! What a bunch of old rope!'

This is a common problem and you just need to bring your emotions into line.

There are various tricks for doing this, and I didn't think up any of them. Here's one: Work on the 'back story' to the service or product you're offering (thanks Michael E. Gerber, and others). Start to focus, not on what your service or product *is*, but what it's *about*.

People don't buy stuff, primarily – they buy feelings. I'm not selling accountancy services for IT contractors. Nor am I selling mere freedom from a tricky, time-consuming chore. I'm not selling relief from a headache, some kind of small-business paracetamol. No, it's far more than that. What I'm selling is *recognition* of *genius*. How? Allow me to explain.

My clients are highly skilled entrepreneurs. They have what it takes to understand really complicated stuff like programming languages, networks and operating systems. Because of their dedication and skill they alone stand between success and meltdown among really huge companies and hospitals and government departments like the MoD. We think everything ticks over nicely most of the time, but they know how close to chaos we really are. They toil there, in the breach. It is their burden, but also their calling. At SJD Accountancy, we do the VAT returns so they can meet their destiny, which is to safeguard western civilisation.

OK, I've laid it on a bit thick. But only a bit. It's kind of true, as well. For quite a few of my customers it *is* true. It *feels* true. So, yeah, it *is* true.

This is the thing about back story. We're into the realms of *meaning*, here, and nobody has a monopoly on *meaning*. It's your call. Your business can mean whatever you want it to mean, and the great thing is, if you're excited and energised and convinced by the meaning of your business, your staff are going to be, and your customers are going to be, too.

Let's say you've taken my advice about the growth in elderly consumers and you're going to start a business in home care for the elderly. Let's say you live in Wales and you've noticed that nobody currently provides a home-care service for the elderly where the carers can speak Welsh. You ring up your mate who works for the council and you ring up your mate who works for the NHS and inside one hour you learn that there are 2,578 housebound, Welsh-speaking people over 70 years of age within a five-mile radius of your house. There are more than 5,000 within ten miles and probably 25,000 in the whole county.

You're *whorfing* big time, but you remain in control and do the smart thing by NOT re-mortgaging your house for the £19,500 it would cost to buy a DynaGran International Care franchise. Instead, you call up your mate who speaks Welsh and who is excellent with old people and who knows half the county anyway and you offer her the post of director of operations and promise to pay her when you get some customers. Actually, when *she* gets some customers. Then you go to the local college and find a presentable 19-year-old Welsh-speaking young person who, as a bonus, happens to be working toward a couple of NVQs that are relevant to home care for the elderly (she's a little bewildered to have actually gotten a job, but you're sure she'll snap out of it soon). And within five weeks of the initial *whorf* your little company has a handful of clients and you and your helper are bustling around, making beds, clipping toenails and setting out the Cheerios.

Now, what is it you are selling? Is it making beds, clipping toenails and setting out the Cheerios? Of course not. Imagine how Mrs Owen feels when your helper, little Bronwen, pitches up and can string two words together in her first language? And not only that but she happens to be the grand-niece of the guy who used to deliver coal round these parts after the war? And not only that but she can tell Mrs Owen (because she's been trained to find out stuff like this) which primary schools have progressed to the county Eisteddfod in the folk dancing and choral singing events?

What are you selling? Is it home care for the elderly? No. You are selling connection. You are offering relief from crushing isolation in a modern, confusing, fragmented world. For lonely individuals you are re-establishing the lifeline from an ancient, dignified culture.

This is absolutely true. How can you not get excited about this? How can you not *believe* in it?

Here is another way to boost your belief in what you have

to offer. Many of us are conditioned to mistrust the profit side of things in commercial transactions. It can feel wrong to take someone's money, especially if you're asking for more than what it cost to produce the service or thing.

You have to stop that. Stop thinking that what you're doing is somehow grubby. What you are offering is not a service or a thing but a solution to a problem. You have been well-meaning and thoughtful enough to come up with this solution, and what you need in return is money, enough so that you can continue to offer the solution, plus a little extra so that you can refresh yourself emotionally and intellectually and look after your family and generally fulfil your own potential so that providing this solution doesn't become a burden and a chore. This should help you to think big about your solution as well (thanks, T. Harv Eker). Because if you were a *really* nice and selfless individual you wouldn't try and limit the number of people who have access to your solution, would you? You would do everything you could to make your proven solution available to as many people in the world as possible. To do anything else would be selfish and mean-spirited, wouldn't it?

I'm not being clever and cynical here. This is a legitimate way of looking at your business and why you are in it. Use this to help get your emotions on board. Your goal is worthwhile. Start believing in it. If you do, everybody else will, too.

CHAPTER NINE

Staying On Course:
How To Run Your Business

We're close to that moment when your business, like some home-made airborne transportation device held together with chewing gum, piano wire and blind faith, has actually left the ground. There are bits hanging off and it's wobbling wildly and the old lawnmower engine is coughing and you're heading straight for the telephone wires and you're all barely hanging on and your hearts are in your mouths and you're cackling like totally crazy people.

What a fantastic moment!

But first we need to go through some things that, hopefully, you did *not* do. I did not do these things, and nor should you.

1. You did not re-mortgage your house or go to the bank or venture capitalists for a start-up loan.

This is the biggest barrier in people's minds about starting a business: where am I going to find the capital? It is not the most important question, but they think it's the most important question. Why?

Because usually when people start out in business they have a very specific picture of how it will look. There is an office, a receptionist, carpets, a few people sitting at desks (doing what, we're not sure yet), the desks themselves (which are rather nice), the computers they'll be tapping away on, the mouse pads, the paper they'll need for printing… oh yes, and headed stationery and cool business cards, a franking machine, a water cooler, filing cabinets, networks, an email system with a firewall, a really, really excellent website, a nice big marketing budget, some pictures on the wall… and so on. That's why it's going to take at least £500,000 to get this business off the ground.

The most important question is not: 'Where will I find the capital?' The most important question is how are you going to get, and please, your first 100 customers? Water coolers and filing cabinets do not make you money. Customers make you money. People dream of all that stuff because they see their business, not as a way of making money, but as an extension of themselves, their style, their values, their tastes. Also, water coolers and so on are the sorts of things the company they used to work for had. Their business would just feel *naked* without them.

Nonsense!

If you've chosen your business well – narrow, cheap, unoriginal and early – you shouldn't need much money to get your first 100 customers.

What's wrong with your kitchen table? For a long time my real office was at 1 Bluebell Close, the three-bed semi in Hemel Hempstead where I lived. I had my admin person in one spare room, the young woman I had in to do payroll in the other spare room, and I had the kitchen table (not that I was around much – I was too busy out getting customers). We were networked up, so there were thick braids of cable snaking through the hallways. You had to pick your way carefully around boxes of forms and stationery. It was chaotic and totally fine.

Yes, some types of business ventures, like property or where you're mass producing a widget or offering a high-end service to fabulously wealthy people, may need some primer capital, but how much? How much, *really*, to get those first customers? All you really need is a phone, a website and a list of people to call. And do you *really* need to borrow it?

Borrowing a whack of money can have dire consequences. For one thing you have to jump through masses of hoops, and fill in mind-numbing forms, and generate intricate and useless business plans, and it's really soul-destroying and dull and you feel like a fraud at the end of it because it's all more or less guesswork anyway. But the real reason to avoid borrowing a whack of money at the outset is because then you don't own the business.

If it's a bank lending you the money then you still own it, *technically*, but if you don't keep up with their repayment schedule they'll swoop in and shut you down. And if you try and get venture capital funding, they are most likely going to want an actual piece of your pie, and then you don't even own the business *technically*. And venture capitalists are very impatient. They don't love your little business. They don't see it maturing and mellowing with time. They want money back, quick. Quick, quick, quick! This quarter! No?! OK next quarter! Show me the money! That's what they're like. It's no fun at all.

Now it may be that's the game you want to play. We saw it in the dotcom days, and it still happens. You've got a great idea – for the masses. The next iPod. A hydrogen car that works. The sort of thing that requires tons and tons of cash well before – usually years before – your first customer will ever materialise. You're going to need world class design, top scientific research and global marketing clout.

Yes, then you do need the venture capital guys. So you call them in, and try and retain as much ownership as you can, but it's not really up to you then. They keep you on because you sort of know how everything hangs together and you've been yakking to the press for the last two years so you sort of *are* the company, in the investing public's mind, for now, anyway. So they make you Chief Vision Officer or something and stick you in a cubicle by the post room. And you wait anxiously for the IPO (initial public offering), hoping wildly that nothing goes wrong with your basically beta product, and you launch on the stock exchange, and it goes OK, and you sell your 16 per cent and run away as fast as you can – with your 2.6million.

Yes, that happens. Like I said, it happened a lot more during 'dotcom madness' than it does today. But it tends to happen with people who've already slogged for years in Silicon Valley, or who worked at NASA, or who are already plugged into high-powered and successful business networks. For ordinary people, just starting out, it is pretty much a fairy tale, and to see it otherwise is just a way to avoid getting on with it and making serious money with what you've got to work with – here, now, today.

I like what Felix Dennis has to say about how to get started without giving up control of your company through debt. He's the super-rich founder of Dennis Publishing (*Maxim*, *The Week*, *PC Pro*, *Auto Express*) who started with diddly squat. His advice, in *How to Get Rich*, is to avoid the sharks and choose the fishes instead. By the 'fishes', he means the many sources of free and useful stuff, goodwill, and assistance that are actually out there if you have the wit to seek, ask, blag and barter.

Dennis's first vision was to produce a comic book. He knew publishing because he'd messed around royally as a co-editor of *Oz*, a controversial hippie magazine. He actually went to jail at one point after a sensational obscenity trial. Anyway, after *Oz* he wanted to get rich, and thought a comic book would be a good way of doing it. And he wasn't going to let the fact that he had no money stand in his way. He got various things, including legal help to set up a company, an office and headed notepaper, by calling in favours, promising to pay later and asking nicely. But the big thing was printing the comic book. It was going to cost thousands (tens of thousands in today's money). How would he get round that? He was a brash, 20-something hippie who'd been to jail over an obscenity charge and he had no money. What leverage would he have with a solid, upstanding printing house?

What he did have was a good relationship with the two guys who ran the well-established company who'd agreed to distribute the comic book. So he asked them to write a letter to the printer, vouching for him and his publishing idea, and assuring the printer that he, the printer, would be the first to get paid when the comic came out.

It worked! Dennis Publishing was up and running.

What great advice: avoid the sharks and go for the fishes. I don't know why he calls them fishes, except maybe it's a reference to Jesus' miraculous picnic, when 5,000 people showed up to hear him speak and it all got a bit late and they were in the middle of nowhere so Jesus fed them, all of them, with what was to hand – five loaves and two fishes.

By the way, did you notice how much *selling* Dennis had to do with the fishes? See what selling can do? Your great speech could be something like: 'Friends, relatives, acquaintances: lend me your cash and carry cards…'

2. Another thing you did not do is invite your mate or spouse to join you as a partner.

Please say you didn't!

If you have a good business idea, keep it to yourself. Why? Two reasons:

1. You need 100 per cent ownership, always and forever, and nothing less will do.
2. Going into business with a friend or spouse will not only kill the business, it will probably kill the friendship or marriage as well, so you're left doubly bereaved.

This is one of the most common reasons for business failure. It happens time and time again. The very notion of striking out on your own, the business idea, the excellent ways you will please your customers and stand out from the crowd, the benefits of freedom and wealth you will enjoy – all these are usually articulated first with a best mate, a trusted colleague or a spouse late into the night over several bottles of wine. And then the ideas are developed and expanded over countless subsequent sessions. You challenge each other's misconceptions and pledge undying allegiance. This will work, you say! Look how well we get along! Look how honest we are with each other!

Me and you against the world!

Thankfully, 90 per cent of these conversations lead nowhere but to a hangover. But in the 10 per cent that do, what happens then is usually disappointment. For one thing, being mates is a whole different ball game from being business partners. The stuff you get from your mate is only a tiny fraction of what you need from your business partner. Here is what you need from a business partner, and these are the only reasons you should ever even contemplate *having* a business partner:

1. They have access to at least 50 per cent of the customers that you want and that you don't have and cannot reasonably get.
2. They have money which you absolutely cannot do without, or they can get access to such money, as much or more than you.
3. They have crucial abilities: they can do, or are willing to do, at least half of the things your business will need to do in order to trade, and which you can't do or are not willing to do (I mean real things, making and doing stuff, not possessing vague qualities or states of mind – *'Oh I'm the ideas person'*)

Even these are not necessarily reasons to team up as business partners. Remember, you need 100 per cent ownership. You can always ask your mate nicely for these things. Or you can offer to buy them, and for a good price. You can *employ* them and pay them well. You don't need to make them *joint owners* of *your* wealth machine. That is a drastic step and should be avoided at all costs. If you want to be rich, you have to embrace this mindset. If you sign up a 50 per cent business partner for no good reason, that means you'll have to sign over 50 per cent of the profits. *To them! For no good reason!* If you want to be rich, such a notion should be scandalous!

And it will ruin your friendship (or marriage). In the warm glow of wine and candles, you and your mate are totally equal (despite the private little criticisms and reservations you have about them, which you confide to your other mate). However, inequalities show up very quickly in the harsh, unforgiving light of business.

Are they as insanely committed as you? Are they as effective as you? Do you rate their brainpower and their problem-solving abilities as much as you rate you own? Are they as reliable as you? Do you trust their instincts as much as yours? It usually takes no more than a few weeks for inequalities to start appearing in these areas, and for the deadening feeling to grow that one of you is carrying the other. In this space resentment starts to fester. In no time at all, crucial reserves of emotional energy are being siphoned off to manage this festering resentment.

What it comes down to is that the mechanics of friendship are entirely different from the mechanics of a business relationship. What friendship is about is 95 per cent *mutual empathy* and five per cent *accountability*. Mutual empathy means we have this joint enterprise in emotional connection: making each other laugh, making each other feel good, trading support and advice and praise and affection. This is the realm of words and feelings and small or large acts of consideration. The five per cent accountability is all about the relatively rare occasions when we actually depend on our friend to do what he or she said they would do to promote or protect our urgent, core interests.

You can see where this is going, right? A business relationship is exactly the opposite. It's 95 per cent accountability and five per cent mutual empathy. In fact, the five per cent mutual empathy is optional, even among business partners. I'll bet there are plenty of effective business partnerships out there where the two partners can barely stand to be in the same room.

I know this is really hard. We're sociable creatures. We like doing things *together*. We want *company*. We want to be able to ring our friends up and say: *'I've just had the greatest idea!'* or *'I've just done the stupidest thing!'* We want to be *loyal*. And we want to *share* with our friends. We can't bear the thought of seeming grasping or mean. And we genuinely want them to have some of the good stuff, too (they can, anyway. You can give them some if you want). But not *ownership*.

With some things, however, it is essential to do them *alone*. This includes going to the loo, picking your nose… and *getting rich*.

3. You did not spend weeks writing up a detailed business plan

The only reason you would do this is if you went to the bank for money, and hopefully I've stopped you from doing that. But some people do it *anyway*. They seem to feel it will help clarify things, work out in advance strategies for dealing with unforeseen circumstances, that sort of thing.

It's a waste of time.

Why? Because analysing the market and the competition, projecting sales, cash flow, and profit and loss, is all *guesswork*. It's imagined response to imagined events. It will be exactly like trying to create a detailed map of a piece of territory you've never seen before. And the form itself will push you into all the usual generalisations, cover-ups, evasions and exaggerations we retreat into when faced with officialdom.

Here is a snippet from an example business plan I found online. This is the sort of thing you're *supposed* to say:

> *'Sales growth will be aggressive the first 18 months as we sharpen our merchandise assortment, size scales and stock levels to better meet our customers' requirements. We anticipate a sales increase of 33 per cent during our second year of operation.'*

Blah, blah, blah.

You're supposed to be getting *away* from hoops, and by deciding to compose a business plan you've just given *yourself* one!

Also, you're going to identify – and start to dwell on – all the unknown bits and all the hard work and niggling questions and it will bring you down. Also it will play to the procrastinator in all of us. You will squander your energy on creating this masterpiece of business planning and it will be a perfect excuse for not actually getting on with it.

Your business plan should be five words long. Ready?

'Get and keep more customers.'

*Now here's what you **do** do.*

You start getting customers and you work like buggery. In that order.

First the customers. A lot of businesses start the wrong way around. They get the financing, rent the office, decorate it, hire the staff, install the fancy customer relationship management software and then sit and wait for the phone to ring. But without customers, you have no business.

My company now has a client base of 9,000. You may never have heard of us, but we're actually in the top 50 accountancy firms by size in the country, and I believe we're the single most profitable.

We're unique because we grew to be this size without ever buying up another firm. We grew organically, one customer at a time. We do this mostly by referrals because we are competitively priced and look after our customers very well. We do what we say we're going to do, for the quoted price, when we say we're going to do it, and we remember enough personal stuff about our customers to have a bit of a chat as well. We're also very clever at marketing and spend next to nothing on advertising (I'll tell you all about this later. It will blow your mind).

As I said, we have 9,000 customers. And this is not nearly enough. There are far, far more contractors out there who do *not* use my company, SJD. That's a big problem for me. I track every new customer. The other day I saw that we got nine new customers in the space of 20 minutes. I was punching the air. I spend a million pounds a year on racing cars. The other day I bought an airline (it's a small airline, carrying mostly freight at the moment around the UK, but it's still an airline). But I still get very excited about nine new customers in 20 minutes!

Here's what I believe about getting customers. There may be only one way of getting a thousand customers, but there are a thousand ways of getting one customer.

So you get some customers, and then you keep them. You have to focus on the customer experience better than anyone else. We do accounting, a cold and bloodless service, right? Wrong. Here's how we get and keep customers:

- **Free face-to-face meetings.** Tax is complicated, so we offer everyone free face-to-face meetings in any city of the UK.

- **Unlimited access to your own dedicated personal SJD Accountant.** No call centres, no outsourcing, no press one for this or two for that. We've banned voicemail.

- **Money-back service guarantee.** All our customers' telephone calls and emails will be answered the same day or we will refund their monthly fees.

As a result, we've won more awards for customer service and accountancy excellence than any other firm in our market.

Once you've got your customers, you start working. This is the *easy* hard work. Probably, at first, you will be the only person providing the service your company offers.

That's what it was like for me. Wednesdays were particularly gruelling. I kept all my Manchester clients, so Wednesdays were Manchester days. I would get up at 4am and drive north, past Manchester to Rochdale, drop off my girlfriend's dog at a friend's place, drive back down to Manchester to my tiny office, spend all day doing my thing for clients and getting new ones, lock up at six, drive north to Rochdale to get the dog and drive back home to Hemel Hempstead, rolling in at about ten pm.

I did that every Wednesday. Yes, I know. Why didn't I get rid of the dog? Or the girlfriend? But that's what happens. When you shift your life to a new direction you get these wild incongruities as things sort themselves out.

Remember, too, I was a national company, with national offices all over the place. So whenever I had a query from anywhere, I would go. Say it was Glasgow. Up at four, drive to Luton. Board plane for Glasgow (thankfully EasyJet had started up by then), arrive in Glasgow, taxi to city centre, wait two hours, no show, back to Glasgow airport, board plane, land at Luton, drive home.

Around this time I also took my tax exams. It seemed a sensible thing to do for the business. You have to revise quite a bit for tax exams, so for a good few months I was studying from six to nine in the morning, then working from nine to five, then studying from six to nine in the evenings, seven days a week.

None of this I minded in the slightest. It was easy hard work. It had to be done and I was doing it for me. This is why business plans are a bad idea, and why you have to just get on with it. If I had known beforehand that I would be putting in these kinds of hours – without any guarantee of getting rich – I quite likely would never have bothered. It's good to take yourself by surprise.

Divide Yourself Up

Starting a business is *easy* hard work, but still the time will come when you hit a brick wall. You'll be working flat out and it will dawn on you that you won't ever make any more money than this unless you 'get somebody in'.

I've made a few mistakes in this regard. One of the first people I 'got in' was my mate and kick-boxing instructor, Richard. It was fine at first. He was a pretty good mate and older than me. He did various things, general data inputting, number crunching and load-lightening. But after a while it became kind of not fine. I felt it took him a long time to finish tasks. This was perhaps no reflection on him, as he wasn't trained or that experienced in what I asked him to do. I saw it as fairly basic, but maybe it wasn't. But there was something else. You couldn't quite tell him exactly what to do. There was an atmosphere of challenge about the place and it got in the way.

Around this time I also hired a young woman called Claire to take over admin. She was great. 18 and eager to learn. Claire conceived and imposed some shape and order to the way the office was run. The system she created had the elegance and simplicity of art. It was a huge relief and released energy into the business.

One day Richard said something to Claire. She was boxing up old printer cables or tidying some godforsaken corner.

'What are you doing that for?' Richard said.

'Because it's got to be done,' said Claire.

'Well, I wouldn't bother. You don't get paid for it.'

I know this conversation took place because of course Claire told me. Not long after that I sacked Richard. It was a bit tense. In fact, we nearly came to blows, which would have been interesting, because I had a black belt by then.

I drew two specific lessons from that experience. One is very simple: don't hire your mates. The other is more complex. Hiring Claire was a good move. Not only was I lucky in finding a high-quality individual, but also I hired her to do the correct thing. Richard's job was vague, Claire's was specific – admin.

As my client base had grown to about 100, I was spending more and more time answering phones, licking stamps and going to the post office. This was hardly a profitable use of my time. So by paying someone £14,000 a year (or whatever) to answer phones, lick stamps and go to the post office, that freed me up to go off and raise the client base to 150. When those extra clients meant I had no time left, I hired another high-quality individual, Julia, to look after payroll. This was one of the simpler services I offered clients, and I could easily train Julia to do it. With Julia doing payroll I was free to go out and grow the client base to 250.

The point is, it's all about dividing yourself, honing what *you* do down, constantly, to the *most profitable* stuff and delegating the rest to others. Here is a simple formula. It will seem obvious, but so many people don't get it right: there's no point taking somebody on who costs more than the extra clients will bring in.

However, although I had divided myself up to a certain degree, I was still the main event as far as SJD Accountancy was concerned. Claire and Julia were good, but if I suddenly keeled over there would be no business. Also, at 250 clients I had hit another ceiling *and* I was working all hours. I had reached that fabled moment in the lifecycle of a business where it was time for me to stop working *in* it, and to start working *on* it.

Michael E. Gerber is great on this topic. In his book *The E-Myth*, he claims that most small businesses fail because their owners never make it beyond that point where if *they* don't do everything, *nothing* gets done – or nothing gets done *correctly*.

I think he's absolutely right. At first if you're a one-man-band or a small business with just you and a couple of staff it's all very exciting, but soon it gets exhausting. It's brick wall time. It becomes an ordeal.

We've all seen it: the embittered garage owner, the raging, alcoholic restaurateur, the shopkeeper who can't stand the sight of his customers. It reminds me of the scene in the movie *Castaway* when the Tom Hanks character finds a sheet of plastic washed up on the beach and hatches a plan to build a raft and set sail in search of inhabited land or a ship. He builds the raft. It's a good one. And he rigs the sail with the skill and patience developed over four years surviving on that island. This is going to be simple, you think. Off he goes, only to get totally hammered by the huge waves that seem to come out of nowhere and rear up and break on the shore. No matter how good the raft is, he's trapped unless he can get beyond those breakers.

This is a good analogy for the small business. The trick is somehow to get out beyond the breakers to the open sea, where there's risk but also big fish to catch. Gerber says you've got to ask these questions: How can I get my business to work without me? And how can I get my people to work without constant interference from me?

What you need to do, he says, is create an organism that is

totally separate from you, that lives and breathes on its own and relentlessly pursues its single goal – to find and keep customers.

The way to do that, he says, is to start engineering your business so that it can be replicated, exactly, 5,000 times over, and can be run by individuals who follow the system. You need to study every function, from the warehouse operative up to sales and marketing, and create easy-to-follow operation manuals so that everyone knows just what to do.

Part of me admires this concept. It's the ultimate franchise model. The title of Gerber's book, *The E-Myth*, refers to the myth that only so-called 'entrepreneurs' – as in, some rare breed of wild geniuses – can be successful in business. The truth, he says, is that anyone can if they put the right system in place. I agree wholeheartedly. Another part of me, however, knows I could never be bothered to go to the lengths he says you need go to, and write loads of detailed operation manuals. I didn't do that. We sort of made it up as we went along.

For instance, one of our clients was highly organised and used to give us his figures on a spreadsheet. I always appreciated how simple and effective this spreadsheet was. Then one day it finally dawned on me that everybody could submit their figures this way if we just designed our forms to mimic his. Duh! So that's what we did.

I don't believe you absolutely must use Gerber's system (which, by the way, you can pay him to learn). What you do need to do is create clearly defined roles in your business, with easy-to-understand standards by which the success or failure of each role can be judged, and hire good people to fill them. And fire them – right away – if they don't match the standards.

I got past the breakers in 2000 when I hired a young, ambitious bloke called Matt. By then I was finding it difficult to divide up any further what I did, so I had to hire a kind of mini-me. Matt was a qualified accountant. His job was to look after London area clients, and he was good – good at getting and keeping customers.

At this point, with good people on board and the business operating smoothly, I faced a choice. I could either sit back and enjoy the £100,000 a year or whatever was coming to me as profit, or I could keep working on the business, taking it to the next level.

Of course I did the latter.

By 2003 I had regional directors in Scotland, Newcastle Birmingham and London, with a client base of around 600. I had settled on a franchise system by then, whereby the regional directors ran their operations and kept a percentage of the profits.

Now, more about hiring good people.

Hiring and Firing

Don't hire your mates. I've said it before, I'll say it again. Friendship is one of life's true riches, so protect it: tell your mates to please go get a job somewhere else. Remember, friendship is 95 per cent mutual empathy and five per cent accountability. Your relationship to employees is the reverse: 95 per cent accountability and five per cent mutual empathy (though that five per cent is optional).

Friends feel that because they're your friends they somehow own a piece of the business. It's just a natural part of the openness and generosity you foster as friends. *What's mine is yours and what's yours is mine.* They don't mean anything sinister by it. They can't help it. The result is that as soon as you begin to focus on the accountability bit, which you need to do from the get-go, they get their backs up. Your relationship isn't *designed* for you to be boss.

Years ago I had a builder to do a fairly major bit of work on my house. He was, *is*, a truly lovely bloke. Honest, clever, fun to have around, cheap, patient and skilled. He became a mate. The problem, as I discovered later, was that he was too nice. He employed his mates and dependents: his brother who was a pretty competent builder but also a bit of a drunk, his sister's teenage stepson, his sister's teenage stepson's girlfriend's uncle, who was going through a bit of a hard time, that sort of thing. He was a mother hen, gathering feckless halfwits under his wing.

Anyway, the work got done, as these things do, eventually. And it was OK at first. Except there was plenty that wasn't quite OK, but he was pretty good at popping round to do a bit of snagging here and there. In fact it got to be that I was apologetic whenever I called him up to come and sort something out. He never minded. 'Ah,' he would say, 'Ricky did this', or 'Bobby did that'. He would smile in a rueful way and fix the problem.

Then about a month later the new upstairs shower started leaking – through the kitchen light fixture. And it wasn't just a drip, it was a torrent. I called him up, apologising. He came round. He looked at this and looked at that. He hemmed and hawed. He smiled ruefully and explained that his brother had done the shower. He shrugged and shook his head, helplessly. He said he would have words with his brother, try and find out what he had done. He was annoyed, on my behalf, but in his mind he was utterly absolved from any responsibility for the cock-up because it was his brother who'd done it. He said he'd get back to me.

He never did. And I didn't call him up and demand that he come round and pull the damn thing out, find the problem and fix it. There was no room in our matey relationship for that – for accountability – just as there was no room in his relationship with his brother for accountability. I lived with that defunct shower for a year before calling in someone else, who pulled the shower out and found a litany of botches.

So don't hire mates. It's not a club you're building, it's a business. So who do you hire? It's not a science, but for a young business you should favour people who are eager generally competent and have a spark. People whom you can train easily and who will hang on your every word.

The spark bit is important, especially for a young business. In the early days I hired a receptionist. She was fine in the interview, but on the day it was like her miserable twin sister had showed up. She was generally competent, but she was a drag. She wasn't exactly rude, not in any way you could pin down, but she was bolshie and bitter and full of resentment and negative energy. She rode that rubbish rollercoaster and was a one-person black hole, greedily sucking in and obliterating any stray enthusiasm. She had an uncanny ability to bring the six or seven other people in the little office down. It was a kind of power she had and she seemed to relish it.

Every lunchtime she would take out a book and hunch over it. One day on my way out I made a bid for some chit chat.

'Hi Jo, what are you reading?'

'A book,' she said, without looking up.

I got angry. It was unprofessional of me, but something snapped.

'I know it's a *book*,' I shot back, 'I was just wondering *what* book!'

She met my eye and lifted up the cover. On it was a photograph of a naked lady performing, shall we say, a certain act about another lady's person. Of the two of us, I'm quite sure that I was the most embarrassed.

That afternoon I 'let' Jo 'go'. Immediately, the atmosphere lifted dramatically. On what actual grounds did I fire her? I can't remember. 'Because you're horrible and nasty and depressing,' would have been the truth, and I would have fought my case all the way to an employment tribunal. The weird thing was that she cheered up when I sacked her. 'Yeah,' she said, 'it wasn't really working out, was it?'

Nowadays there is a lot of nervousness about unfair dismissal. Employers should fight back. If somebody's no good, fire them. Do it quickly and cleanly. Whatever it takes to get rid of them, within the law, do it – right now. I've seen a lot of small businesses hobbled by horrible, nasty people, or by unreliable people, or by incompetent people, or by thieving people, any of whom the owners are too timid to sack. These people do untold damage. They sap morale among other staff and they erode your self-belief. In all my years in business I've fired my share of people, and we've only been through one employment tribunal, which I won.

It does work the other way too, by the way. Hire a bright, enthusiastic spark and the whole atmosphere lifts. But I have noticed that bad people are a lot denser, and bring everybody down quicker.

Hiring people is a gamble. You have to trust that it will all work out, but be prepared to act quickly if it doesn't. I have to put a lot of trust in my regional directors. As franchisees they have a fair bit of autonomy. We provide support and marketing – customers – and they hand over a chunk of their profits. And I've sacked a few.

One guy was stealing from me. He was a meek and mild accountant, who I'd made regional director in Birmingham. I began catching this whiff of rat. The profits from his office just weren't what they should have been. But I couldn't work out what sort of rat it might be. I had a look at his books and didn't see anything out of the ordinary at first. Then I noticed that a sizeable chunk of cash was going to a particular company I didn't recognise. I looked it up at Companies House and saw that it was my regional director's company. It was hardly sophisticated fraud – we're not talking *Ocean's Eleven* here – but he'd managed to siphon off £15,000. I went to Birmingham to confront him. His wife crumpled but he blandly denied it, even after I'd pulled out the documents and connected the dots – all two of them.

I got my money back. We came to an arrangement in return for my not calling the police. Then he was 'let go'. I don't know what he's doing now. I'm not a rancorous person. Perhaps he's rich, or perhaps he's in some special limbo for meek, mild and bent accountants.

Another regional director in Scotland launched an outright mutiny. He just changed the name of the company and walked off with all the clients – my clients. That was too much. I sued and won.

It's a gamble. Hiring people just is. You can either burden yourself and your company with all sorts of failsafe controls, or you can bet on people who seem good and let them get on with it. Remember Claire, the admin girl? She moved on to doing accounts, and of course she was good. She got the last SJD franchise I gave for central England, and she's now bringing home something like £250,000 per year (imagine if she'd gone to university!) .

And remember Matt, the whippersnapper I took on to cover London? I decided to buy his franchise back from him in 2009. It would be wrong to disclose how much this 35-year-old was able to hold out for, nor would it be discreet to speculate as to which Caribbean island he was able comfortably to retire to as a result. Let's just say he did alright.

Show Me the Money

Another essential thing to get right, early, is getting paid. You would be amazed at how bad many young companies are at this. Cashflow is as crucial to a business as blood is to an animal.

Do you know what an embolism is? It's very bad news. It's a bit of something in an artery, like a blood clot – something solid that should not be there – that can get stuck and block the flow of blood to a vital organ. A shortage of cash, even a temporary one, is exactly like an embolism quietly working its way toward your brain.

You could be doing great on paper. You may have achieved £100,000 in sales this month. But if your customers take 60, 90 or 120 days to pay you, you're going to run into real problems paying your staff, your suppliers and meeting all the myriad operating costs in the meantime. Many, many theoretically profitable businesses go to the wall this way.

You have to be a bit hard, which is difficult for business novices. In part it's because it feels grubby and awkward, this demanding payment. It's also a breed of laziness. All the good bits – winning the business, delivering the service – are fun and exciting. You get a buzz from that stuff. To then have to chase payment is an afterthought, and a downer, like clearing up after the party. Being hard is not nice for the novice, but you're in business now. It's not like university – you're in the real world, and the real world is tough at times. That's why you learn so much from it.

It usually plays out like this. You ring up a customer.

'Hi,' you say cheerfully. 'Just checking to see that everything's OK with the service we provided.'

'Hello!' says the customer, warm and delighted to hear from you. 'Yes, thank you, the service was excellent. We shall certainly be using you again.'

'That's great to hear. Thanks! Um… I just wanted to let you know that we sent you the invoice a couple of weeks ago. Did you receive it?'

'Did you? Oh, right. OK, sorry about that. Leave it with me and I'll have one of the guys chase it up. We'll send you a cheque next week. Is that OK?'

'That's great! Thanks so much!'

Job done, you think. That was easy.

But two weeks go by and no cheque.

You pick up the phone again. Except this time you are tense and nervous and apologetic.

'Hi there, it's me again. Just to let you know, we don't seem to have received that cheque from you. Sorry…'

And your customer, who has been doing this for years, starts filing her nails and says: 'No? I can't believe it! I'm going to go down right now and give the accounts department such a bollocking. What's the matter with these people? I'm so sorry. Look, just leave this with me, and I'll get back to you.'

'Oh, thanks ever so much,' you say, shaky with gratitude and relief.

And another two weeks go by. This time you pick up the phone and you manage to sound a tad miffed. Again, you explain. This time, however, your customer seems to have no recollection of the previous two conversations, and insists that they haven't received any invoice from you whatsoever. So you raise another invoice and send it.

One week goes by.

You call. This time your dander's up.

'Look,' you say, 'you need to pay me now, or… else.'

Your customer seems to have undergone another personality change. This time she's eager and conciliatory.

'This is so embarrassing,' she says. 'I'm writing a cheque, right now, from my own account, and I'm going to walk out of the building and post it to you myself.'

Another week goes by. Then an envelope arrives. You tear it open. It's a cheque from your customer. But it's not signed.

Six months after you sent the initial invoice you begin court proceedings. Two weeks after that your customer goes into administration.

Two weeks after that you go into administration.

This happens all the time. The only way to prevent it from happening is to embrace in your heart from the outset that getting paid is an essential part of the service which you have been good and kind enough to provide. If you don't get paid, promptly, there will be no service. Furthermore, you need to make getting paid a major part of the opening negotiations.

Start with: 'We require full payment up front.'

If they moan you say, 'Sorry, company policy.'

If they flatly refuse – and you'd be surprised how many won't – you insist on half mid-way through with the remainder payable immediately upon completion.

If they say, 'Don't be daft. We'll pay you after 30 days like we do everybody else,' you have a choice. Take the business or walk away. If you're minded to take the business you need to weigh up very carefully whether you can actually afford to fund their business – because that's what you're doing – for an entire month, and quite likely more. Can you? Do the maths. Put that GCSE to work. If you decide you can and day 31 comes without a cheque, call in the bailiffs – on day 31.

Be especially aware of this if you're supplying corporations, like the big food retailers. They may have standard terms, like 90 days. Three months is a long time to wait. You may be able to get financing to see you through, especially if you have a purchase order from Wal-Mart to wave at the bank manager, but do the maths. You may have a million pound purchase order from Wal-Mart, but it's going to cost £997,000 to fulfil it. With the bank charges and interest you need to ask whether it's worth the business or whether you're actually running a charity.

Another thing you could do is delegate the money chasing to people with the right skill set. Make sure you have somebody really evil in your accounts department, someone who curdles the milk of human kindness just by walking into the room. You know the sort I mean: you're on the phone with them and venom actually drips out of the receiver. Poach a couple of solicitors' receptionists, or pick up an early retiree or two from HMRC. Put them in their own cubicle, shut the door to muffle the snarling, and hang up a sign saying 'Special Projects'. Stern telephone calls are really just sounds, but they work. People will go to just about any length – including writing a cheque – to avoid another such call. Then you can go and do the fun stuff.

Cashflow. Overlook it at your peril.

CHAPTER TEN

Final Year Exams:
How To Market Your Business
for Free

I've really been looking forward to this bit. If there is one thing in the whole book that's the 'special sauce' or the 'secret recipe', it's this. And on the face of it, it's not very earth-shattering. You've probably heard it, or parts of it, before. If you're looking for astounding, hidden mysteries, you may be disappointed.

And yet it *is* astounding. Here it is: You don't need to spend money on advertising. You don't need focus groups or expensive brand awareness campaigns. All you need to do is string a few sentences together in plain English and be able to create a web page.

If you can't make a webpage yourself (and they're really surprisingly simple to do) find a friend to do it for you or pay the minimal amount of money it takes for a proper web designer to create your page.

Let me repeat myself, in case I haven't made it clear just how simple it is to get free marketing for your business. All you need to do is write stuff and make web pages. That's what we do. Our advertising budget is practically nil, and yet over a quarter of all new customers come to us because we're clever at using the web. I said before that we're in the top 50 accountancy firms by size in the country, but we are in fact still a small fish in a big pond. For now.

Had you ever heard of us before you picked up this book? Probably not. And yet our web presence is huge. We've built up a bank of 3,000 different web pages which attract a million visitors each year, and a very satisfying percentage of those visitors become customers. And guess what? We're not web wizards. We don't know anything about SEO (search engine optimization). We don't even have a clue how Google actually works. We just know how to make it work for us.

Information is King

Consider this diagram.

The Buying Cycle. 98 per cent is light grey, labelled 'Customers researching'. two per cent is dark grey, labelled 'Customers buying'

What it shows is that, if you were to freeze the frame of the Customer Kingdom at any one moment, what you would be lucky enough to witness, amid all the growling and stalking and pouncing, is that of 100 people, 98 are researching and a measly two are actually buying.

The researching phase is important and you can't short-circuit it. This is where we as customers sniff around, have a bit of a reccy. We've experienced the pang, the desire, or the perception of a need, and now we're checking out how that pang, desire or need can be satisfied. We may still only be working out what that pang, desire or need is, let alone how it can be satisfied and how much we're willing to pay.

The research phase has always been part of the buying cycle, but it used to be a lot more complicated, expensive and time consuming. Let's say you became interested in spratlins. You've heard of spratlins and you think they might just do the trick for you. So you ask your barber, and your neighbour and your work colleagues and your mates down the pub. But nobody really knows anything about spratlins round where you live, so you get on the phone and ask friends, relatives, anybody you can think of.

You become a bit of a spratlins bore. You go to the library and they've got a couple of books on spratlins, but they're quite scholarly and way too detailed. Next time you're in the newsagents you notice a magazine, *Spratlins Monthly*, so you buy it. Most of the articles are for spratlin experts and the more you read the less you understand, but at least there are a few ads for spratlin manufacturers and resellers so you ring a few up and ask them to send you some spratlin literature. Which, after a week or so, they do.

You pore over this literature and you start to build a picture of the different sorts of spratlin solutions available out there and how they're packaged and priced. You have a few detailed conversations with spratlin salespeople and get a feel for warranties and after-sales service. Finally, about a month after the spratlins idea first popped up, you're ready to buy.

That was in the Olden Days. Now of course we just type *spratlins* into the Google search bar, hit 'enter', and the whole wide world of spratlins opens up before us. Or at least we hope it will.

The Internet has dramatically altered the research stage of the buying cycle. It's all revved up now. Everybody has consumer expertise at their fingertips. You see it most in healthcare. Patients go to their GPs crackling with knowledge. They're only there to get a second opinion, at best, or to tell him what prescription to fill out. I've seen parents whose children suffer from an obscure condition becoming, in the space of a week, far more expert on that condition and its treatment options than paediatricians. In offices up and down the land, big-hitting specialists and consultants are being put through their paces by in-the-know cancer sufferers. It's a nightmare for these guys.

Is all this information people have correct? Is it true and accurate? It doesn't matter. What matters to consumers is the feeling of power, of being in control, which having that information gives them.

The first thing anybody does now when they want to buy something is Google it. There are exceptions. When women go shopping for clothes they tend to just go and browse. It's the whole experience of discovery and surprise, of immersing themselves in the environment so the magic can take hold. For women, to approach clothes shopping first by Googling would seem anorak-ish and weird.

Also food shopping. We tend to just go to the supermarket, unless we're researching something rare or unusual, like yolkless, pasteurized egg whites. But for anything that isn't a routine purchase, anything that departs from the well-worn path to the watering hole, we fire up the web browser. We purchoogle. What have you purchoogled in the past month? Sim cards? Landscapers? Trampolines? Graphic design? Wet rooms? Home-care for the elderly? Is it safe to holiday in Sri Lanka?

Sweet FAQ All

So far, so what, right? OK, this is the good bit. How much of your purchoogling in the past month has been rewarding and fast? In how many cases did ten or fifteen minutes of purchoogling answer at least some of your stupid questions and make you feel more confident as a potential buyer of the product or service? My guess is, not a lot. My guess is that in many cases, especially where you purchoogled a service that hasn't been commoditised yet, you felt more stupid and baffled than you were before and gave up to go and do something that stopped you feeling stupid and baffled.

If this has been your experience, you've had an important glimpse of a remarkable thing. The internet has been with us for years now, and we all feel like old hands at it, but the truth is that very few companies – and this goes for big, sophisticated companies too – very few companies know how to use it properly for marketing.

By and large companies are still bringing old-fashioned and obsolete marketing strategies to the web. In most cases, no matter how flashy a company's website is, or how beautiful and subtle and tasteful, it is usually just a clever and expensive adaptation of a Yellow Pages ad. It answers certain questions which *the company* thinks are important: here's who we are, here's how long we've been around, here's what we do, here's what's so great about us, here's how much it costs and here's how to buy. What's wrong with that, you ask? What's wrong with it is that these are not the questions that *98 per cent of the customer base* is asking at any one time.

Ads, whether they are in the Yellow Pages, or banner ads on websites, or in magazines or newspapers, or on television, all address the two per cent of customers who are *ready to buy*. For the other 98 per cent who are *researching* they are just clutter and noise. That's why advertising in general, especially where you can't escape it, like on TV or the radio or on billboards wherever you look, is such a *drag*. We're not *there* yet, man! Companies spend billions and billions of pounds and squander huge creative and intellectual efforts on *annoying* their potential customers.

It happens with websites too. Let's say you've been thinking about building a conservatory. You need the extra space. But your big concern at the moment is whether it's going to require planning permission. You have no idea. Your neighbour put up a conservatory last year but you can't ask him because he's a tosspot and you haven't spoken since his teenager scratched your car two years ago and he wouldn't do anything about it.

Right now, for you, the planning thing is a make or break

issue. Your local council, Cheeryside Borough Council, is notoriously slow and pedantic and if you need to get planning. It's frankly not worth it. So one morning when the boss isn't looking you Google 'conservatory planning permission Cheeryside'. And what you get is three or four ads up at the top for companies like Cheeryside Conservatories and The Cheeryside Conservatory Company. These you ignore because, from your point of view as an information seeker, these are just chancers. You don't want an ad, you want an answer to your question. There are also a bunch of ads down the right side of the page, which you also ignore because you know these are just lower-grade chancers, chancers with even less to offer.

The first proper search result, however, catches your eye. You read: '…click to expand Submitting a Planning Application... Cheeryside Borough Council…' So you try that. And what you get on the opening page is a big red notice saying:

'**Please Note: This website is no longer being updated since 01/04/2008 (Local Government Re-organisation in Cheeryshire). For up-to-date council service information, please visit <u>Cheeryshire County Council </u>website.**'

This you are not really minded to do. But you do. And you get the Cheeryshire County Council website, which has pictures of happy old people on it, but nothing about planning permission for conservatories. You click on 'planning' and get lots of stern notices and detailed forms to fill out, but nothing about conservatories. You are beginning to feel that special neuralgia on the left side of your face that always crops up in the presence of boredom and pointlessness. You gamely type in 'planning conservatory' on the site search tool and you get 741 results, all of them minutes of this or that committee meeting, the most recent in 2001, and all utterly unintelligible.

Back you go. Back, back, back, back to the original Google search page. The other search results look equally arcane and off piste. Thinking 'What the hell?' you click on Cheeryside

Conservatories, and you are treated to a true feast of colour, punctuation and word-processing razzmatazz:

GREAT SAVINGS ON CONSERVATORIES!
'25 per cent OFF!'
Yes it's true; Save 25 per cent off our custom built CONSERVATORIES ordered this week!

Whether you're looking for a new room to relax or more space for work or the children to play in, **CHEERYSIDE** *custom-made* **CONSERVATORIES** are designed to enhance and fit perfectly with **YOUR HOME!**
You can choose from a great range of **DESIGNS** and styles to suit you and your home!
Plus, we have many **FINISHING TOUCHES** from ceramic floor tiles, centre fan lights and a range of classic or contemporary furniture for those **FINISHING TOUCHES**.
Our **CONSERVATORIES** are manufactured and installed to the *highest specifications* and come fully guaranteed, for total peace of mind for *many years to come*!

You lower your hurting face to the cool desktop. Quietly, you begin to sob.

This is not a particularly extreme or exaggerated example, especially for small, local companies. Bigger companies have websites that look much better. They pay good money for web design and for copywriters to come up with taut, polished and flawless prose about their company. But it is still aimed at the two per cent who are ready to buy. That makes it, for 98 per cent of visitors, taut, polished and flawless drivel.

Another example of this is Frequently Asked Questions (*FAQs*). In theory this is a great way to talk to your customers, but how many times have you clicked on the *FAQ* section and found there nothing that, as far as you can make out, anybody in their right minds would think of asking? That's because the company didn't set it up as the *FAQ* section, they set it up as the

COB section (*Covering Our Backside*). For the majority of visitors, this offers sweet-*FAQ*-all.

The internet is amazing. For next to no cost, for pennies, it allows you to reach people all over the world who might have an interest in what you have to offer. It is the single most ground-shifting invention in media terms since the printing press. And yet hardly anyone out there has grasped how to use it.

Get Down With the 98 per cent

So what is the answer? Dead simple. Start talking to the 98 per cent. You don't even have to rip out what you've already invested in. Just start talking to the 98 per cent.

There is a bit of a trick to this, but not a huge one. You have to begin to think like your potential customers. You have to understand them and start giving them what they want, which is information. What do they want to know? I don't know… they're your customers! Talk to them. Pay attention to what they say. Make a list of the questions they're asking. Use the words they use.

Then you write simple articles that answer those questions and you publish them as separate pages on your website.

There it is, the big secret weapon.

We've been doing this for years now. Acting on some instinct or other – I think it's called common sense – I sat down and wrote an 80-page guide for people toying with the idea of becoming IT contractors. It covered everything I could think of, VAT, payroll, expenses, double-entry bookkeeping, the upsides and the downsides of switching from permanent employment to contracting, the lot – all of it based on my expertise and also what I was gleaning every day from my customers. That became the basis for what is now more than 3,000 pages of useful information for contractors and would-be contractors, whether they are my customers or not.

What is the point of that, you ask? Why is an accountancy firm acting like an expert on IT contracting? Well, because we are, actually, and also because we now have 3,000 web pages out there getting down with the 98 per cent. A million people a year use us as a resource while they make tricky life decisions, like whether to go independent or not. They're learning all kinds of useful information. They're getting answers to their basic questions and their expert questions and the questions they may not even have thought of asking yet. And when the time comes for them to maybe think about outsourcing their tax and accounting, who do you think is going to emerge as a rather obvious starting point?

Us.

Remember I said before that there may be only one way of getting a thousand customers, but there are a thousand ways of getting one customer? Well, there are 3,000 ways, too. And each of those 3,000, if they're any good, can be reeling them in as fast as billy-o.

Is it all really that simple? Of course not. But it's almost all really that simple. There are two standards you need to apply to make it work for you.

1. Set the page up so that Google can find it easily for people who are searching, and
2. Write good articles.

The Clever, Eager, Faithful Dog

You need to drive traffic to your pages. In order to do that you need to appear right at the top of the search results whenever anybody searches for something relevant to you. By right at the top, I mean in the top five results, and certainly not in the paid-for 'sponsored links' at the top or side. We're all getting much better at Googling now. Gone are the days when we sadly trawled through page after page of results in search of that gem or nugget. If we don't find what we're looking for in the first page now we usually refine our search or give up.

We're in the realms of SEO here, Search Engine Optimisation. Now don't worry. I'm not going to get technical, largely because it's beyond me. What I do know, however, is that you don't have to shell out good money to SEO boffins for them to write whatever magical algorithms they write, or to perform their keyword wizardry, in order to drive your web page up the search results. All you need to do is write great, interesting, easy to understand and relevant copy, label your page correctly and honestly, making sure it matches the content.

Nobody really knows how Google works. It's like a clever, eager, faithful dog. You give it a vague search term and off it goes, tail wagging furiously, nose to the ground, tearing around in wider and wider circles and bringing home things it thinks you'll like. It does what you tell it to, but it seems to know when the content of a page is disguised to be relevant to your search, but isn't really. How does it do this? No idea. Except that they've probably got 2,000 boffins over in California who do nothing but write clever, eager, faithful dog code.

Anyway, here is how you can help that clever, eager, faithful dog.

You need to create a helpful web address for the page – also known as a URL. Let's say Cheeryside Conservatories has taken my advice and is starting to talk to the 98 per cent. They've done a bit of research and have come up with a great little article full of tips on how to build a conservatory that doesn't require planning permission in Cheeryshire. They write the article and send it over to the guy who does their website, instructing him to put it up as a new page. He says sure. But they haven't told him exactly what address (URL) to give the page. So he makes it up, and it could be anything, but probably something like this:

www.cheerysideconservatories.com/
17a2nh1085n*per centn4.html

Why? I don't know. I told you, I'm not technical. That's just what a lot of URLs look like. But they don't have to. You can call your web page anything you like, as long as it isn't taken yet. So the Cheeryside guys, having read this book, get clever and tell their web guy to call the page this:

www.cheerysideconservatories.com/
guide_planning_conservatories_cheeryshire.html

You can do that. There may be a better one, but that's better than the gobbledygook before, and it alerts the Google dog right away that you may be worth investigating.

Second, you need to create a good 'meta title' for the page. This is what appears in Google searches as the first line. If you don't compose something specifically, Google will choose whatever is the first line or two. So if you've composed a load of rubbish, like *'Here at Cheeryside Conservatories we have been assisting our valued customers for 27...',* the Google dog might cock his leg and go off after a better scent. You've got to cut to the chase, as the information seeker sees the chase. How about:

Cheeryshire planning rules for conservatories

Next comes the page (meta) description. The Google dog brings searchers this to help them understand what's on your page. Take some time on it, as it could reel searchers in. Again, if you're in obsolete marketing mode, you're going to end up with drivel, like:

The pages of history are littered with examples of...

When you could just as easily have had:

Top tips for building a conservatory without planning in Cheeryshire

When building a page you can also add a few keywords behind

the scenes. Again I have no idea how Google uses these, but they help. You could add things like:

Conservatories, planning permission, tips on building regulations…

To support this, make sure your copy faithfully echoes these words. Like I said, Google seems to know if you've done it haphazardly or if you've really thought about it.

Finally, if you do any searches on 'SEO' in Google you'll read lots about linking. This simply means getting other people to link to your website. There are even companies that will, for a fee, gather links for you and do all the hard work. My advice is, ignore them and instead focus on writing great copy. This way people will naturally link to you. If you force it with 'link-farming' and gather hundreds of phoney links, Google will sniff them out. They might add some 'click-through' value in the short term, but it won't last.

Now as I'm sure you can tell, I haven't been on one single course about Google. We just got to know how it works and how to give a helping hand to that clever, eager faithful dog. I also have a very clever marketing consultant friend, Julian Carnell, who is a total monster with this. A big part of his job is just to think like our customers, to really understand their stresses and pains, and to write interesting, helpful and friendly articles to help them. Google seems to pick up on his passion, so we get a lot of visitors coming to our sites. It's getting to the point now where new customers kind of complain that while they were in the research phase, hemming and hawing, checking out this or that angle on the whole contracting thing, SJD seemed to be the *only firm out there* talking to them. They couldn't actually *get away* from us. That is a problem I think I can live with.

Julian does a lot of thinking about what new questions our potential customers will be asking, as well. For instance we sussed that one of the biggest shifts in Britain's industrial make-up now looming on the horizon is nuclear power. For a few years now the government has been manoeuvring and clearing the way for a new generation of nuclear stations. The estimates are that as many as ten new ones could be built over the next decade or so, each costing something like a billion pounds.

On top of the new stations needing to be built and run and maintained, there are also 19 old nuclear power stations at the end or coming to the end of their operational life. These need to be decommissioned and deconstructed, which is just as big and expensive a job as building them. All this is going to lead to thousands of opportunities for self-employed contractors in IT and engineering. Any contractor worth his or her salt is going to be considering the nuclear sector as an option.

So Julian rang up the press office at Sellafield, who were delighted to speak to him, got a few basic facts, and wrote a nifty little article. So now if you do a Google search for 'contracting nuclear' or 'how to be a nuclear contractor', you will find this article, from SJD Accountancy, in the top five results. If you search 'becoming a nuclear contractor' the top two results are SJD Accountancy (any one company is only allowed two results per search).

What is an accountancy firm doing, advising people on how to be a nuclear contractor? It's nothing if not audacious.

So you don't need some fancy SEO consultant. I'm sure that what they do is very clever and might actually bump your site higher up the search results – temporarily – but it costs money. Plus – and this is the key thing – it still leaves you with the problem of what the visitor will find once they click on your site. If it's a load of old cobblers it doesn't matter how many innocent clickers fall for the trap. My advice is to love and understand your customers, genuinely try and help them, write great copy and forget about fancy clever marketing tricks designed to hoodwink Google. If you do this Google, Yahoo and Bing will love you forever. Remember, unlike an advert that requires paying for continuously, a great webpage will last forever.

Quality Content

Like I said, Google is very clever and seems to know if you've written quality, relevant text. If you try and short cut the process, Google will spot this and not list you on the vital first page.

I find this the fun part, but I know that for many people it's terrifying, like being forced to learn academic stuff again. Relax! This shouldn't make you nervous. Anybody can write quality, relevant text for their customers.

Let's start from the beginning. What should you write? What you should write is what the 98 per cent will want to read. And what will they want to read? That's easy: useful answers to their questions. Make a list of these questions. Start with the most basic, entry-level questions that people will feel stupid even asking and go to town on them. Remember, you're talking to the 98 per cent. If you feel stupid just writing the answers, you know you're starting at the right place. I'll go back to the home-care example. Here are some good introductory questions:

- What is home care?
- Who uses home care?
- Who provides home care?
- Why use home care?
- How does it work?
- How much does it cost?

Then you move up to more intermediate-level questions.

- How often do carers visit?
- What are carers able to do?
- What won't they do?
- How does the fee structure work?
- What financial help is there for home care?
- How far will carers travel?
- Can we choose when they come?

And then you tackle the more involved questions.

- Should Gran get home care or be in a home?
- How qualified are carers?
- How good are they at dealing with dementia, Alzheimer's, etc?

If you've covered the basics you can then branch out and answer any question your 98 per cent might be asking, or might realise is a great question once they see it posed. The question does not have to be about you or your expertise. If you can get your hands on useful, honest answers, you deserve to be capturing that space as much as anyone else.

- How can we keep Gran from starting a fire?
- What is dementia and how can you detect it?
- How hard is it to install a stair lift?
- How do you convert a garage into a granny flat?

So that's what you write: answers to good questions. Each question forms the basis for a short article, between 200 and 400 words, and each article gets its own web page on your site. Take care over the *heading* of each article. This is the 'sell', and will give you grist for the URL, the meta title and the page description. Don't be afraid to label it aggressively: 'Top tips for', 'The essential guide to', 'Secrets of', 'How to', 'Six ways to' – these communicate clear value to information hungry visitors.

Can you promote yourself in these articles? Yes! You must! But not in a clunky way like Cheeryside Conservatories. In his article on Becoming a Nuclear Contractor, Julian spent around 230 words addressing that question in a useful and honest way before seamlessly moving the discussion onto ground favourable to SJD: becoming a contractor and how to set up a limited company, which links in to services we provide. Also, this web page that you create specially for this article will have your name, contact details, buttons leading to other parts of your site and a list of other relevant articles as well, so you can afford to be a bit subtle and stick to the question that drew the visitor in the first place.

You're not going for a Pulitzer Prize in journalism, though. Think of what you're writing as good propaganda. Its job is to attract, inform and sell.

You can also refer to your competitors by name, if you want. As long as you don't slander them. There are several possible advantages to this. One is that you come across as even-handed and not afraid to mention competitors – even if you're actually cut-throat and grasping. Another is that potential customers will be grateful that you gave a fuller picture of the options available to them. Also, your web page will come up even if people are searching for the competition.

Success will come if the article creates a little spark of gratitude and empowerment in the visitor. It doesn't have to be a major thesis. It just needs to be a worthwhile two and a half minutes, leading to other worthwhile two and a half minutes, leading on sooner or later to a decision to buy.

How to Write it

A funny thing often happens when people who are not accustomed to writing are faced with a blank page. Bizarre personality changes occur. This happens because they feel they ought to adopt some sort of 'style' because, if they don't, what they write will be plain and naked and exposed. So they dig around in their memories for a style they feel is correct or attractive and they come up with all sorts of odd things.

Normal straight-talking people suddenly become Professor Wienerschnitzels and erect edifices of prose that are so complex and abstract they are all but impenetrable. Or they become Winston Churchills and unleash a blizzard of lofty, rhetorical flourishes. Or they take cover behind snazzy but meaningless jargon. Or they insist on telling jokes, constantly, even if they are not that good at telling jokes.

Don't do this. You don't need to. What you want is actually plain and naked and exposed writing. It might be hard at first, like learning how to go around without a toupee, but it's necessary if you want to connect with the 98 per cent. Here are my top tips for writing copy that will please customers and help Google:

1. *Write like you talk.* Pretend your mate has asked you a question down the pub, and you're telling him the answer. Down the pub you would naturally do this in the most simple and economical way possible. Your brain does that automatically. Now you have to teach yourself to write that way.

2. *Just answer the question.* Get straight in there and do it. It's not an after-dinner speech, where you have to start with an amusing story. No throat-clearing exercises, like, 'Since the dawn of recorded time, mankind has made provision for its elderly…'

3. *Talk to your customers.* People often forget who their audience is and start writing as if their competitors or their teachers were looking over their shoulders, which pushes the prose into distracting cleverness or jargon or general nonsense.

4. *Organise your answer and stay focused.* Make a little list of the five or six points you want to make and put them in a logical order. Then start with the first one, write a few sentences on it, and move on to the next until you're done.

5. *Use short sentences.* They work better. Use them.

6. *Get somebody else to proof it.* Find the most grammatical person in your office and have them read it. Your writing needs at least one extra pair of eyes, and preferably more.

They must correct any errors, but also flag up anything that doesn't make sense. These articles don't need to be great writing or high art, but they do need to be fault-free. Errors will make you look sloppy and lazy and dumb.

7. *Be helpful.* If you've found links to helpful sites (not to your competitors, though) put them in.

8. *Judge your audience.* If you repair surfboards you can probably use more slang and wacky prose, but if your customers are solicitors you need to keep it more formal and sober. The text should always be simple and clear, though.

Be warned. Writing simple, useful and effective articles can be time-consuming. It's not easy making something complex, like tax and accounting, seem simple. Coming up with the question, doing the research and writing a good piece all takes time. But practise makes perfect, and it does get easier.

There is another clever tactic you can use. Google Adwords is one of the best inventions ever. You set up an account, pick your keywords and then decide how much you're willing to pay, per click, for Google to direct clickers to your page. The more you're willing to pay, the higher up the rankings your ad gets placed. The higher the search traffic for a particular keyword, the more costly it is to secure a prominent place. I don't suggest you pay any money at all to get clickers, but you can use the system to see what keywords are really driving traffic at any one time. Then you use that intelligence to tailor your next web page accordingly.

So there it is. Our big secret weapon: how to market your business effectively for nothing, or next to nothing. Am I worried that my competitors will start copying what we do? Not at all. Very few companies actually get the combination right. Some *may* be able to make the intellectual shift from the two per cent to the 98 per cent. Some *may* be able to forget what *they* want to talk about and start focusing on what *customers* want to talk about. Some *may* be whizzes at using keywords and creating web pages that are easy to find. And some *may* be able to write simple, effective and useful material. But I haven't seen anyone else yet who does all these things together as well as we do.

Most companies can't let go of obsolete marketing strategies. Marketing types seem to *have* to place ads. They're addicted to it, even though it costs huge amounts of money and delivers, for the most part, few tangible benefits (if you are contemplating spending thousands on advertising it probably means you don't really know who your customers are yet, and you're paying through the nose to find out).

Remember, display-advertising, or big, flashy banner ads on websites, only speak to the two per cent – the tiny minority who are ready to buy, right now. Plus, these ads only stay alive as long as you keep paying for them. As soon as you unplug the life support they vanish without a trace. You can see why it's like an addiction. And marketing types keep feeding their addiction because, if they don't, their advertising budget will be cut and they will have nothing else to do.

Many companies also just can't be bothered to go through the process I've described here, so they hire PR companies or external webmasters to do it. I think this is a big mistake. Why? The biggest reason is that they won't know your customers like you do, so they can't write for them like you can. For them, it's just not coming from the heart. They may be able to produce polished and fancy prose. Next to theirs, your lovingly crafted pieces might seem plain and naked and exposed. But for the amount of time you'll need to instruct them and change what they've written, you might as well have gone and done it yourself.

External agencies will also try and fob you off with blogs and tweets and news feeds that use content generated from news agencies. I've seen competitors do this. So any news story with the word 'contractor' in it gets uploaded to your site automatically. You end up with 'Nine contractors murdered in Nigeria' or 'Council sues building contractor', ridiculous stuff that neither you nor your customers are remotely interested in. On top of all that, it costs a lot of money.

Do it yourself. The best things in life, and business, are free – but require effort. Find out what the 98 per cent are asking and give them answers in simple, effective prose. It works.

CHAPTER ELEVEN

Entrepreneurial Masterclass: MBA Not Required

So you've done the easy hard work, your business is up and running and everything is a great success. You've got loads of customers and you're keeping them. Your staff are busy in their clearly defined roles. Your market share is increasing all the time.

You made it!

You are now ready for the Simon J. Dolan Entrepreneurial Masterclass on what, as an entrepreneur, you should do now, how to keep airborne and keep on climbing. You do not need an MBA for this. In fact, it's probably better if you don't have one because, if you have an MBA, this will seem too simple and unsophisticated to be taken seriously.

I say Masterclass, but really it's just a few pointers.

You Don't Make Money Sitting in the Office

Are you still in the office? Why? What are you doing there? Are you afraid that if you don't show up every day the whole thing will start to malfunction? That business will start to drop? Then you need to go back and read the chapter on dividing yourself up.

Or maybe it's because you spent the last five or ten years working like buggery at the office, and even though you kind of sense that you're in the way, the truth is that now you don't actually know what to do or where to put yourself. So you turn up every day and immerse yourself in detail and demand reports on this or that or draw your staff's attention to this or that trend you've spotted while surfing the web – and generally make a nuisance of yourself. Ask yourself: is what I'm doing right now making me money? Sitting in front of your screen, checking trends, making PowerPoint presentations? It's very easy to fill an entire day with stuff that ultimately doesn't matter.

It's time to let go. You have more important work to do. There is more money to be made and you won't earn it sitting in the office. Get out there and stretch your legs. Lift your eyes to the horizon.

What makes money? Yes, customers. But before that? Before there were customers, what was there? Ideas. Ideas make money. And you don't get ideas sitting in the office, feeding off and distracting yourself with the process that you created years ago and that is now working fine and doesn't need you. Think about it: the idea that gave birth to your business, to all these people running around doing stuff, to all your customers, to this comfortable and attractive office – it didn't come from this office. It came from somewhere else, from outside the office. It happened before there even *was* an office. So it's time to stop pestering your operations people, switch off the computer, put your jacket on and *leave*.

Go get some more ideas!

The best way to get good ideas is to talk to interesting people who are doing interesting stuff. Reading is a great way to learn and to get fresh perspectives. I read – a lot. But reading is a really low-bandwidth activity compared to talking to people. A 20-minute chat with somebody can open up whole new solar systems of possibilities. If you want to get to grips with a complex topic you can buy some books and spend the next three months reading, or you can find an expert and take him or her out to lunch. It's just the way our brains work.

I mentioned that recently I invested in an airline. This happened after exactly that sort of chat. I was flying to a race in Dijon, France. The thing about motor racing is that the tracks are often in the middle of nowhere and unless you're willing to waste an extra day or two driving, it's better to charter a small plane.

So I was sitting next to my race-team manager, Sam Hignett, who is also one of the owners of the aviation company. My racing team had been a customer of theirs for some time, but this was the first time I'd had a chance to chat. We talked about the business of little airlines, how they work, what you do and how much money you make. It was all very interesting. 'Hey,' I said, 'if you ever want any investment let me know.' A couple of months later he rang me up. 'As it happens,' he said, 'we're thinking of expanding. Perhaps you'd like to come in?' So I did. I'm now a part owner of Jota Aviation Ltd, and we're going places.

I'm not suggesting you neglect your business. There are whole books written about people who took off and then walked out of the metaphorical cockpit, started drinking cocktails with the cabin crew and didn't notice that the craft had gone into a tailspin until after it was too late. You have to keep an eye on growth, on profits and on the customer experience. But it shouldn't take up all your time. If it does, you have some more work to do *on* your business. When that's done, start booking time away.

Act Fast

New ideas can be for totally novel and different business ventures, or they can be flashes of brilliant insight on where to take your business next. Either way, make sure you act fast.

Have you ever heard of something called the Pareto Principle, or the 80/20 rule? It's named after an Italian economist, Vilfredo Pareto, who did some clever maths in the early 1900s to demonstrate that 20 per cent of the people in Italy at the time held 80 per cent of the wealth.

The 80/20 ratio must have some inherent attractiveness because ever since then scientists and management gurus have stretched it to make all kinds of points, like 80 per cent of your sales are generated by 20 per cent of your staff, and conversely 20 per cent of your staff will cause 80 per cent of your problems.

Scientifically I don't know if it holds water, but there's one variation of the Pareto Principle that I find particularly riveting. It has to do with getting things done, as in new product launches, or setting up new companies, and it goes like this: 80 per cent of the end result is accomplished 20 per cent into the scheduled programme. Is that true? Who knows? It's a question that would keep quasi-academics writing in business journals for decades. But it feels true. It certainly makes you look at a new project in a more gung-ho light, doesn't it?

Julian, a great friend of mine who happens to be the world's best marketing consultant, has a couple of great lines. One is: nothing takes longer than four hours. Once in a meeting somebody asked what our sales plan for next year was. We looked at each other and shrugged like a couple of teenage cretins.

'I dunno. Kind of like what we're doing now?'

'Only more.'

'Yeah, and better.'

He also says: no plan should be longer than one side of A4, which apparently was the extent of Norman Schwarzkopf's battle plan for Desert Storm in 1991, launched to push the Iraqis out of Kuwait. I don't know the ins and outs, but it seemed to work. Just one side of A4. You can have quite a few scribbles on it, but just the one side.

When Sam rang me up and asked if I'd like to invest in Jota Aviation, I could have taken at least a couple of months to research it. I could have slogged my way through boring market reports (also known as guesswork), I could have showed up at little airports up and down the land, mystery shopping and snooping around. All this I did not do. I sat down with Sam and had a look at the books. I checked out cash flow, current customers and what plans they had. It seemed fine.

I'm sure it took less than four hours. As a result, we're a couple of months ahead in our business plans, doing the marketing, getting the licenses and all the other necessary stuff. Do those two months matter? In the long run maybe, maybe not. But acting fast does harness your enthusiasm better. It's like after Wimbledon everybody's mad on tennis. Kids are out playing against the side of the house. Men and women are whacking balls for the dog. The mania lasts for about two weeks. It's a real force, but unless there's something real to rig it up to, it dissipates.

I'm not saying you should switch your brain off completely. There has to be an element of rationality to it. But you should strictly limit the amount of time you're going to spend researching. Say you want to develop a new type of oil. You've spent a bit of time checking it out. You know there's a market for it. Somebody else is doing it. You believe you could do it well. What more is there to research? You're always going to find reasons why it's a bad idea.

Focus on Sales Over Cost-cutting

Yes, you need to keep an eye on costs – overheads – and the biggest overheads are people. Overheads walk on two legs, goes the saying. However, if you have to worry about and focus on something more, sales or overheads, pick sales.

I say this because the amount of costs you can cut from your business is finite. Theoretically, you can cut your costs down to zero (I know this is impossible, that's why I said *theoretically*). Further than zero, you cannot go. However, there is *no* upward limit on the amount of goods or services you can sell – if you've chosen your business well. That's why sales is always more important than cost-cutting. It's a mindset you need to embrace.

People focus on cost-cutting because it's easier. It's easier to pick up the phone and bother your stationery supplier, haggling for another two per cent off, than it is to pick up the phone, call a stranger and sell your product or service. We know which one is easier, but which one is better for your business? Sales.

Prepare for Luck

In 2007 the government passed a little law that was, from our point of view, very handy indeed. I won't go into it but basically it did away with managed services companies (MSCs), which handled tax and national insurance for clusters of contractors. With the demise of MSCs, contractors had to sort out more of their own accounting. As a result, thousands flocked to us. Yes, it was a significant windfall. Our client base went from one thousand to four thousand in a year. Our business quadrupled.

Sure, we got lucky. But remember what Seneca said: 'Luck is preparation multiplied by opportunity.' If we didn't already have a great company providing a great service it wouldn't have been a fantastic bit of luck, it would have been a boring bit of legal news. And if we hadn't been adaptable and fleet of foot we wouldn't have been able to absorb that tsunami of customers, we would have been swamped by them.

But absorb them we did. With pleasure! And we were then able to enjoy the special magic of customer-led business growth. As the hard-working Davie Jones discovered back in 1964 with The Mannish Boys: gigs get gigs. It works in business, too: customers get customers. It's magic! The bigger you get, *the bigger you get.*

Good Failure, Bad Failure

Business ideas fail. Businesses fail. It happens. We've all our share of it. I believe failure can be good. There is no better way of learning fast, of learning how to do it correctly – next time. Nothing drives home a complex suite of lessons faster and more durably than landing on your ass. Failure is an essential, natural and inescapable part of learning. Failure ultimately leads to confidence, clarity and commitment.

But I do think that there is good failure and bad failure. Good failure leads somewhere new and better, while bad failure is just failure, and doesn't lead anywhere except to itself. It's Nowheresville, end of story.

You mustn't ever plan to fail, but our brains are hugely complex and sophisticated and we can afford to be not so dogmatic about this. You don't plan to fail – obviously! – but one part of your complex brain can be working on this problem: if I *do* fail, how can I engineer it so that it's a *good* failure and not a *bad* one?

In business it's about careful deployment of your capital. By capital, I mean *capital* capital, as in money, but also the other very important types of capital that a good business depends on.

8   *Social capital*: If this venture fails are you going to be able to talk to important people again? Suppliers? Talented staff? Mentors? Your husband or wife? Will anybody trust you again? Have you been honest? Have people followed you into this with their eyes wide open?

•   *Intellectual capital*: Is this the only idea you have and will ever have? Or are there others bubbling away on the back-burner? If not, and this is the only idea you have and will ever have, will the failure spell the end of it, or might there be other forms it could take?

•   *Spiritual capital*: This is a bit of a catch-all heading but it means the *oomph* left in you after the venture hits the buffers. How quickly will you be able to pick yourself up and try again? Can you face it? Is your enthusiasm going to return or will you have boarded the rubbish rollercoaster for the duration, and become an exclusive dealer in blame, resentment and self-justification?

Engineering good failure is all about making a rigorous appraisal of how you are deploying this capital. You have to make sure that if your venture fails you're going to have some of it left for the next one. And the *capital* capital, the money, is not necessarily the most important, contrary to what most people seem to think. If you've got enthusiasm and good ideas and big, solid relationships the money can be an incidental thing.

There is a very clear parallel here with gambling. There are bad gamblers and there are good gamblers. We can picture the bad gamblers, those disastrous wrecks tumbling out of the bookmaker's. Less prominent in the public mind are the quietly successful professionals who make a pretty good living at gambling. These men and women know the game, know what they can afford to lose and make calculated risks on big rewards. If they lose big, which they sometimes do, they just start again at another table next week. Bad gamblers may know the game, but their risks are not calculated. They will bet everything based on a couple of emotions, usually hope and a misplaced sense of *entitlement* – basically, that God *owes* them *this* time. What drives them is delusion and desperation.

I think the way most people view the risk of failure in business is coloured by the garish myth of the entrepreneur, which paints him as some sort of half-mad dreamer who mortgages the house to the hilt and cashes in his wife's pension for some hare-brained get-rich-quick scheme. That's not what I did, and it's not what you have to do. As I said at the beginning, being an entrepreneur is not about entering some hellish gulag of slog, panic and financial ruin.

It's about working hard and building something carefully, piece by piece, that is yours.

Advice to Parents

Parents. It's time to talk turkey. I believe that the A level-University treadmill is actually harmful. I think it gets in the way of young people leading a fulfilling, productive, independent life. I've come to the conclusion that we've basically run out of ideas as to what's best for our kids.

Is the road I've gone down the sort of road you might wish your son/daughter to take? If the answer is no, it would seem I still have some work to do. If you haven't been convinced that getting a degree is at best an expensive way of putting off getting a job and, at worst, is actually harmful and stunts young people's imaginations and prospects for personal growth and autonomy, then it may be something to do with me, personally.

Fine.

Let's deal with that.

I Am Not a Monster

I suspect that a lot of parents shy away from encouraging their sons/daughters to start a business – with the express intention of getting *rich* – are for three main reasons. One is that they believe it's a mug's game, that it's just a hellish gulag of slog, panic and financial ruin.

That one I've dealt with as much as I can.

The second is that they worry about their sons/daughters becoming money-heads. I understand that. They worry that their kids will turn out to be shallow, grasping and morally deformed. They worry that the bald pursuit of lots of money is an inferior goal on every important level – morally, spiritually, intellectually and culturally. They are perfectly happy for their son/daughter to become wealthy as a side effect of pursuing goals that our culture praises, like celebrity or careers in law and medicine. And they dream of their children becoming wealthy by sheer luck, through the lottery or inheriting a pile from some unknown wealthy aunt. But to actually *set out* to become rich, for its own sake, is just somehow… wrong.

I don't get it. I really don't. I believe we have a *dysfunctional* attitude to wealth.

I'm quite rich. How rich am I? You can check that out in the Sunday Times Rich List.

And I am not a monster. I'm just normal. I don't feel any different in my own skin than I did when I was a photocopier salesman in Manchester. I don't look at people and think: *I'm richer than you*. Nor do I look at people and see only money opportunities or money hindrances. I carry around a bulging suitcase full of foibles and anxieties like anyone else, including those hard-as-nails entrepreneurs you see on TV. I love my kids so much it hurts and I worry that they'll be OK. I have to work at being a good dad and husband and I don't always get it right. Friends and family are really important to me and sometimes, like everybody else, I find friendships and family relationships tricky and confusing.

All during the years of building my company I did not think exclusively about money. What I thought about, obsessed about, was doing a good job – in the same way that most of you obsess about doing a good job.

I'm just normal. Millionaires are people, too!

However, it *is* nice being rich. Money is not everything. I know that. Money isn't more important than love or health or intelligence or art or anything else you value. But money *is* great. It doesn't buy happiness, but it buys space and time and fun and beautiful settings and pleasant experiences and the best medical and legal assistance available. I've thought about it and I don't think there is a single downside to having lots of money. Except maybe that you might have certain friends or family members who think it's weird that you're rich and they're not and this becomes a problem for them, but that's their problem.

Running your own business and being your own boss is great, too. It's easy hard work.

I'm not a money-head and not one super-rich person I've ever met is either, so why should your son/daughter become one? We set the patterns for our kids' behaviour. It's really scary, but the fact is they soak up everything from us. What we say, what we do, it all goes straight in and gets stored for repetition later. You can teach them to be wise and civilised and public spirited, to appreciate beauty and to be kind and clever – *and* to want to be rich. There is no space limit on what you can teach them. You don't have to ditch one value if you want to cram in another.

The third reason why parents shy away from encouraging their kids to go for wealth as a goal in itself is that they worry that having loads of money will turn their sons/daughters into feckless halfwits. They look at their irresponsible youngsters and think: Crikey, imagine the damage they'd do to themselves if money were no object! Look at what fame and fortune does to people! Look at Pete Doherty and Amy Winehouse! Everything that is suspect and bad in their natures – their egocentrism, their thrill-seeking – will pop out of the box and run riot!

Well… maybe, but…

OK, David Bowie got into cocaine big time in 1974 and spent two years in a state of delusional, skin-and-bones paranoia (although he never stopped working and he made the album *Young Americans* during this period – OK probably his worst album, but an album nonetheless). But the pressure to go down that road seems to be pretty high in the world of pop stardom. And he snapped out of it fairly quickly.

Somewhat closer to home, in relation to what we're talking about, the publishing tycoon Felix Dennis bravely admitted that he blew more than a hundred million dollars on booze, drugs and prostitutes over ten years. He'd think nothing of shelling out thirty or forty thousand for a single night on the town in London, New York or Hong Kong. Eventually he got sick and had to be hospitalised and he started to clean up his act, but not before a lot of irrevocable damage had been done to his relationships and his health.

They say power corrupts and so people assume money must corrupt as well. It doesn't. For every rich, feckless halfwit there are many more that live well and modestly and cultivate healthful habits. Like me. There is nothing intrinsically corrupting about money.

For instance, I like race-car driving. So I do that and enjoy it. Race-car driving is a complex and highly expensive skill, but it makes me very happy and the fact that it's expensive hasn't corrupted me.

On the other hand, I believe there is something intrinsically corrupting about poverty. It breeds despair and resentment and destructive thought patterns. If somebody feels the urge to get into altered states and abuse drugs and alcohol and break the law they're going to do it whether they have money or not. If it isn't champagne and fluffy white powder in the company of the most beautiful women money can rent, it'll be crack and Diamond White under the flyover.

What Are You Teaching Them?

In his book *The Secrets of the Millionaire Mind*, the memorably named T. Harv Eker says we all have a wealth thermostat deep inside us that regulates the amount of money we allow ourselves to have. This wealth thermostat is set subconsciously, as a result of the conditioning we receive from our family and from the community around us while we're growing up. Everything goes in and sets that thermostat precisely.

Phrases, like 'fat cats' and 'filthy rich', which pack an emotional punch, whether we're attuned to it or not, go in. Sayings like 'money is the root of all evil' and 'an honest day's work' go in. Images or stories that link wealth to greed, privilege or criminality go in. Behaviour like parents sneering at the neighbours for buying flash new cars go in. Attitudes like the glorification of 'the common man' and hard work as an end in itself, or outright hostility toward 'The Rich', all of this goes in and sets our wealth thermostat.

That setting then determines what we aim for, and we always get what we aim for.

We may *think* we like the idea of money – who doesn't? – but the reality we create around us is actually determined by our deeper feelings and attitudes. In money terms, it's the wealth thermostat doing its job. And if by chance we come into more wealth than the thermostat's set for, an alarm goes off and we lose it. The reasons for losing it might *appear* to be beyond our control, but old T. Harv says no, it's the wealth thermostat kicking in, and that, at the end of the day, we control what we want to control.

Now, I'm not sure about my wealth thermostat, but my balderdash thermostat is a highly sensitive instrument and I think T. Harv Eker is absolutely right.

If you don't want your son/daughter, or yourself, to be rich, why not?

If you do, then promote the message. Wealth is good. Wealthy people are good for society. *You can be wealthy.* I tell my kids all the time: if you want to get rich you have to set up your own company. Kids are total sponges. They will learn what you teach them. So if you want them to be rich, start shaping their minds to be rich. This isn't sinister. You're shaping their minds anyway. You might as well get organised about it. If you project an ambivalent attitude to money, they're going to have an ambivalent attitude to money.

Line in the Sand

Parents, I want to address a potential catch-22 you may feel is lurking in my argument. For the Messing Around phase, you need jobs. That's because jobs are the easiest way to do a few years of self-directed messing around. There are other ways, but for most people jobs are the best way. And it is true that a lot of even entry-level jobs require a certain amount of scholastic achievement, like a few GCSEs, especially English and Maths. These days more and more jobs, even at entry level, are requiring degrees. That's because employers want to make sure they're not hiring complete dunces, and being able to tick a few qualification boxes is an easy way, they think, of separating the wheat from the chaff (employers are not geniuses, either).

On the other hand, what employers really want, what they are always desperate for, even in recession, are people who can get on with a job. People who can understand instructions, process information accurately and do useful stuff with it. Useful to the employer's organisation, that is. What they don't need are clever, pampered babies. We know this. It's common sense. Nobody wants clever, pampered babies.

So how are you going to make sure your son/daughter fairs OK? Let's start with this. They have to get two GCSEs. Maths and English. End of. No A level or degree is required to gain your approval.

As an employer, I would say there is something impressive about that. A kid would have my full attention if she came up to me and said:

'I got two GSCEs, the most important ones, and not only that, I got an A* in each, plus a letter of recommendation from the teachers. That's it. That's my line in the sand. I didn't do any more GCSEs because I'm not going to university. I'm not going to university because I want to be wealthy and have a good time. Also, I was kind of busy playing in my band and working at McDonalds. I'm actually a supervisor at McDonald's and I've learned masses about fast food, supply chains, government regulation, the paying public, how to get along with people higher up and lower down, what you can fake and what you can't, and I've already got £1,230 saved to plough into my first venture. But McDonald's is now doing my head in and I need to diversify my experience for the next couple of years, so that's why I want to be a warehouse operative, and here's your two bloody GCSEs. Now give me a job.'

Wow!

Sorry, as an employer I was fantasising a bit there.

Do you see what I'm saying? Two GCSEs. Or maybe it's three, or four. Or maybe it's two, plus ten hours a week of voluntary work with a relevant organisation. Or maybe it's no GCSEs just yet, because maybe your son/daughter already has a full-time job they like, but understands that getting those GCSEs should probably be done before they are 18.

Or not.

Whatever!

Just flex your parenting muscle in a targeted, clever way, so that your son/daughter can get started on their self-directed Messing Around phase. The sooner she gets to it the better. The self-directed bit is key. It only works when it's self-directed. Suddenly your useless lump of a teenager is wazzing around on this home-made motorised skateboard contraption (I'm talking figuratively). They made it themselves. That's why the lawnmower's in bits. The noise is deafening. They're spewing blue smoke. They keep falling off and skinning their knees. They're swerving all over the place, but it doesn't matter. They're off.

They're putting all this energy into something because they've understood what they want to get out of it. You might think it's misguided, but keep it to yourself. They're off, they're learning. They're going to learn more useful stuff in the next six months about themselves and the way the world works than they did in the last ten years listening to you. I'm sorry.

But there's no jobs!

That's the big excuse, isn't it?

There's no jobs! I don't see any jobs! Do you see any jobs?

Picture the person saying this. He may still be a teenager. His mouth is turned down, like the tragedy mask in theatres. His eyes have that look of grievance and injustice. He knows there are no jobs, for a fact, because he has spent every evening for the past six months moaning about it with his 92 'friends' on Facebook.

Yes there are jobs.

I heard on the radio that there are now nine hundred and something thousand young people out there between 16 and 24 who are 'NEETs' – Not in Education, Employment or Training. I don't find this all that surprising, judging by the calibre of the 16-to-24-year-olds I've encountered recently. But there are jobs. Yes there are. There are loads of businesses out there, heads down, doing their thing, needing hungry grafters. Seek and ye shall find. I own one of those companies and I need hungry grafters. Are you a hungry grafter? I'll give you a job. If you can get yourself into my office – without breaking the law – and capture my attention (within the bounds of decency) for five minutes, I'll more than likely give you a job.

Education of the Soul

Two more things about education. First, I know education is important. Ignorance and stupidity are really bad for people. Bad for children and young people. Bad for taxpayers. Bad for the country. Kids should emerge into their mid-teens literate, numerate, confident and intellectually hungry with a growing appreciation for how the world works and some moral backbone and – why not? – a bit of spiritual and cultural sensibility.

That's the education of the soul. It's what equips you to live a good life. The biggest influence in this regard is families. School plays an important part for reading and writing and maths and getting along with people and some useful knowledge, but for many kids it becomes mostly hoop-jumping from GCSE-level up. For most people I don't believe the A level-university treadmill adds anything at all to the education of the soul.

Second, my advice is for entrepreneurs, people who want to be seriously rich and live exciting, independent lives. Sorry, not people who *want* that – who doesn't? – but people who *intend to be* that. People who have it *in* them and are *going to do it*.

Yes, but is my son/daughter cut out for this?

Good question. OK, here's the thing. I don't think *everybody* can do it. Just as I don't think *everybody* can handle a job that involves rare skills and a lot of pressure. Some people take a lot longer than others to grow up. Some people never do. And some people just like the feeling of safety that comes with employment and that's the way they want to keep it.

There is nothing wrong with that.

But what I've tried to show is that there is nothing mysterious or particularly difficult about starting a successful business. I believe many more can do it than actually do. Look at the group of 17-year-olds goofing around every night outside the convenience store wearing those stupid hats. Then think of all the 17-year-old, stupid-hat-wearing losers making nuisances of themselves every night around the country. I believe that at least 40 per cent of them – no, more, 50 per cent or 60 per cent of them – could make it without too much trouble. Maybe not become millionaires right away, but certainly successful and independent in a business of their own. And that has nothing to do with forcing them into university. They have to have a good Messing Around phase, though. Just *messing around* isn't enough.

Think of your own son or daughter. If he or she is a teenager you're probably close to despair. Are they lazy? Are they really? What about when they find something they like doing? Are they lazy then? Laziness can mean all kinds of things. It can mean you're not sure it's actually OK to do something you want to do. It can mean you're scared you might fail. It can mean you tried it once and it didn't work. It can mean you're not sure what to do next, or even where to start.

If they're a teenager you may be in a pitched battle over A levels and degree courses. You may be pulling your hair out because you know they can do it, but they just don't *try*. My kids are still little but I have friends with teenagers and I know how frustrating it is. I know people who are literally counting the *weeks* left before their child is 18 – *only 73 to go!* – and therefore technically, legally able to be chucked out. I remember my *own* parents' frustration over me.

But I would say that this is potentially a *fertile* situation.

Teenagers are awkward because what they really want is independence and autonomy. It's their job to want those things. They may make bad choices and choose silly or harmful ways of expressing their proto-independence, but they're just doing their *job*. When I do an inventory of the really big people I know, the ones with rare talents or the powerfully spirited, they were almost all of them awkward teenagers, real headaches or worries or disappointments to their parents. That's because they had a tough job: they had to work out what their *place* was in the world, how they *fitted in*, and it wasn't obvious at all.

If your son/daughter doesn't see the point of higher education or other activities (of the sort my parents used to call *constructive*) are not soaking up nearly enough of their energy and attention and all they think about is boys, or girls, and scoring beer and smoking dope and hanging out, then why not pander to this drive for independence?

Why not help them harness it? As long as they've got a few GSCEs (Maths and English) why not suggest they forget about university and A levels and get a job? The idea might seem weird to them, especially if they've been brainwashed into thinking that they'll be losers if they don't go to university and get a prestigious career. But they might find the idea of money attractive, and they might like being treated like an adult, and they might enjoy mixing with other adults and having a laugh. Jobs aren't always a complete drag. Some are quite fun. Remember?

Fine, you say. So they forget about university and get some crummy job, with a view, eventually, to starting a business. But have they got what it takes to start a business? What if we do them a huge disservice by hoiking them off the university treadmill when the university treadmill is all they're cut out to do?

Here are some basic questions you can ask about your son/daughter:

1. Are they basically self-motivated in at least a few *constructive* pursuits, like school, music, a job, sport or a hobby of some kind?

2. Do they like having money?

3. Do they have a realistic perception of money? (Or have you *trained* them to expect clothes, toys, money and treats whenever they start whining?)

4. Do they sort of know and take an interest in what's going on around them?

5. If they hit a brick wall do they give up or do they persevere?

6. Do they look after themselves or do they need to be nagged, for instance, to get up on time, brush their teeth, etc.

7. Do they mix OK with people?

8. Do they try new things and learn from them?

If you answered 'yes' or 'sort of' to at least four, no, three… no, two of these questions, then *congratulations*! You have an *extremely* high-functioning teenager!

The truth is, I don't know. The other truth is, it's not that hard to set up a good business. The other truth is, *it doesn't matter*. I believe the sooner young people get out there and start making money, acquiring skills and experience and learning about themselves and the world, the better, whether they decide to be an entrepreneur or not. They can always go back and get an academic or professional or vocational qualification later. I did.

I got a really tough tax qualification while I was extremely busy getting my business off the ground. It was hard work, but *easy* hard work.

How You Can Help

Start early. Please, please, when they are young, at least outline to your children the possibility of being their own boss, of setting up a business and making a lot of money. Throw it into the mix, along with medicine, law, nursing, whatever. And resist the temptation to lace it with all sorts of cautionary hokum.

'You mean I could set up my own business, Daddy?'

'Oh yes, dear. Anybody can.'

'And would I get rich, Daddy?'

'Well, you might, but only if you drink the special potion that turns you into a horrible, grasping slimeball like your Uncle Tarquin.'

Kids start getting curious about careers from a very early age, and yet most parents don't even mention starting a business and getting rich. So when these kids grow up and start thinking about it as adults, when they start dreaming about it, wishing they could do it, they've already made too many choices that seem to cut that option off. By then, they feel it's too late.

This is madness! It must stop! Shut off the sweet, loser propaganda of Que Sera. It's true that whatever will be, will be, but the future *is* ours to see. Our thoughts create tomorrow. You're in charge. If you're not, somebody *else* is going to be. Obviously we can't predict everything about the future. Certain things are probably beyond our control, like foreign governments or the global economy – although there are plenty of people who make it their business to try and control those things, too. Natural disasters, certain genetic diseases, freak accidents and sudden political upheavals are, may be, beyond our control. But that leaves a huge space left over where we are in the driver's seat whether we accept it or not.

Next, talk to your children about business. Not the economy and what a weird, frightening, out-there force it is, but *business*, as a thing people can do well or poorly, like football or art. Make it normal. Talk about it and how it works – supply and demand, profit and loss, quality, customer service. I'm not saying become a total bore on the subject. You don't have to brainwash them. But when you're out and about, at McDonalds, for instance, you might introduce the idea the McDonalds is not actually, or at least is not *just*, some miraculous, God-given fountain of pleasure and excitement, like the beach, or puppies, but is actually a business that somebody thought up and made lots of money from. Again, you don't have to analyse it to death. Just bring it up and let it drop. Kids may find it quite an interesting revelation.

So that's the early days. What about now? Say your son or daughter is a teenager and a bit lost. Address the issue head on. Is education, the whole ethos and setting, doing good things for your teenager, or bad things? Is it increasing their confidence and knowledge or is it quashing and confusing them? If it's doing bad things, take charge of the situation. Encourage them to get a job. Or you might suggest they check out college and maybe get a vocational qualification, like I did, and then get a job.

The big thing is giving them *permission*, reassuring them that it's *OK* to do something else, something that turns them on, that harnesses their energy. Your vital input is helping them see the bigger picture, feeling good about the bigger picture, that getting a job is not failure, but just the next step toward them becoming free and independent adults. Teach them about the art and science of Messing Around.

You can help them get a job. It's OK to do that. They don't *have* to do *every last thing* themselves. Don't erect barriers before they've even started. If you think about it, you may have a ready network of friends and relations spanning a variety of industries. Use it. You're allowed to do that for your kids. Make introductions. Grease the way, like my mum did.

There are jobs out there. Ignore stories about rising youth unemployment. The companies who advertise jobs in the papers or at the Jobcentre are only the top bit of the iceberg. There is a whole secret world of frustrated managers and business owners who would give their right arms for willing grafters, but who don't have the time to search properly for them, or haven't worked out how to do it yet because they have other urgent priorities. They hope, somehow, that the right person will find *them*.

Busy hotels and restaurants always need willing grafters. That's why the friendly, motivated people cleaning your hotel rooms and serving you breakfast have odd accents – because the only willing grafters the hotel managers could find are economic migrants.

Think big. Think laterally. Maybe there is not a single job in your town or city because the Labour Government screwed it all up. OK, get your son/daughter out of there for a while. Maybe you have friends or relations in another town or city that your son/daughter could go and stay with. Ask them. Set something up. A change of scene, meeting new people, getting to know a new place, all this is a hugely broadening experience for young people.

What if your son/daughter has a business idea already and wants to start? Wow. That's exciting. Why not? There are plenty of successful teenage entrepreneurs out there. I wasn't going to give examples, in case it depressed you, but I changed my mind. I think you need to know.

Here's one: Adam Hildreth. In 1999, when he was 14, this West Yorkshire lad set up an early social networking website called Dubit from a computer in his bedroom. It became a marketing resource for companies like Coca-Cola, who used it to convene focus groups to help them market to young people. At 16 he quit school – which he couldn't stand – to become MD of the agency. He did that for the next few years, leading Dubit to become one of the most visited teen websites in the UK.

In 2004, the BBC named Hildreth, then 19, as one of the UK's 20 richest teens, with an estimated net worth of £2 million. In 2005 he left Dubit to start another business, Crisp Thinking, which developed software to protect children from online groomers. At Dubit he saw a lot of pervs infiltrating the site trying to lure young people either to meet up in person or to exchange pervy messaging. The software doesn't look for obvious keywords, but other telltale signs – conversation patterns, typing speed, use of grammar and punctuation.

Here's an even better one – or a more depressing one, depending on your point of view. This one's from America. You may even have heard of him: Cameron Johnson. Not to take anything away from Hildreth, but Johnson's story is somewhat less of what you might call a purely dotcom one, and more of a classic – and therefore universally repeatable – entrepreneurial story. It also really shows what even a child can do with the right input from parents.

For Christmas in 1994, when he was nine, Johnson got a computer. He used it to create invitations for a party his parents were throwing, and got so much positive feedback that he started making, and selling, greeting cards. His parents also let him set up his own bank account and taught him how to manage money. They also bought him a few stocks and shares, which he enjoyed playing around with. By the age of 11 he'd amassed a few thousand pounds. His company was called Cheers and Tears.

At the age of 12 he offered to buy his younger sister's entire collection of Beanie Babies, a popular brand of stuffed animals. She had 30, and he offered $100 for the lot. Deal! Then he sold them all on eBay, and made $1,000. Smelling an opportunity, he called up the manufacturer, Ty, and negotiated wholesale rates for the dolls, and started selling them on eBay and on his Cheers and Tears website. In less than a year he banked $50,000.

That provided the seed money for his next venture, 'My EZ Mail', a service that forwards emails to a particular account without revealing the recipient's personal information. He hired a programmer to write the software and within two years 'My EZ Mail' was generating up to $3,000 per month in advertising revenue.

It gets worse. In 1997, he joined forces with two other kids to create Surfingprizes.com, a weirdly ingenious kind of online advertising company. It was a pyramid selling scheme in which members would get paid to use web browsers that had annoying online ads. If you downloaded the browsing software, you got 20 cents an hour for putting up with the ads. Advertisers could be sure of a captive audience, and users who got a new Surfingprizes.com customer also got ten per cent of that new person's hourly revenue. Johnson told *Forbes* magazine: 'I was 15 years old and receiving checks between $300,000 and $400,000 per month.'

When he was 19, he sold the company name and software. He hadn't even graduated from high school yet and he was a millionaire. He certainly hadn't taken a degree.

So what if your kid has a business idea? My advice is that, unless it's totally delusional or illegal (*I want to be an international arms dealer!*), get behind it. It may be hard for you to think objectively, especially if you've spent the last four years raging at them about homework and turning off lights and keeping their room tidy, but try. It doesn't have to be *the* ultimate, winning idea. It just needs to be broadly sort of realistic, maybe, and *theirs*. It's a start. Have faith. Offer assistance. If you're on speaking terms, offer your superior knowledge and experience to move their idea to a realistic starting point. If you're not on speaking terms, or if it degenerates into a slanging match about who's in control, enlist help from another adult to do this.

You can also help with seed capital, or help them find it. Not that you'll pay for their business. It's got to be a *business*, after all, or they won't learn from it. You can help with *anything* – marketing, admin, introductions, references, advice, a shoulder to cry on, whatever they need.

Hang on a minute, you say. That all sounds like way too much work for me. Does it? What I would say is, how much work and effort gets squandered, and how much stress and strain and pointless, negative energy gets generated, in trying to push unwilling young people onto the A level-University treadmill and keep them there? Proper parenting is hard work, whichever way you cut it. Wouldn't it be great if you could work *together* on something during these challenging years, on something you *both* see the point of?

What a wonderful thought.